HER MAJESTY THE QUEEN

Queen Mary
of England

A Life and Intimate Study

BY

Kathleen Woodward

GEORGE H. DORAN COMPANY : NEW YORK

PREFACE

THE work of Queen Mary is inseparable from her life and personality; in that her life is one long service to her country, the quality and completeness of that service but the perfect expression of her character.

So this book came from what was, at the beginning, an intention to write only of Her Majesty's work.

Throughout my enquiries I have been altogether unhampered; I went to all parties, to all classes, seeking my material where it was best to be found, and preferring always the living, human sources to which I was admitted by Her Majesty's approval of my early object.

For the benefit of those who may find this book too personal, I would remind them that the essence of the power of Queen Mary is in her personality; and "Everybody knows how constantly history has shown that personality may be a force as powerful in the world as projects and ideas," said Lord Morley.

For the graciousness I have met during this work, and for the help I have received, it would indeed be difficult adequately to express my thanks.

The Marchioness of Crewe and Lady Cynthia Colville first commended my purpose to the Queen; without their help the book could not have been written. The Marquis of Crewe, K.G., in the midst of many cares and at a period when affairs of State made more than the usual demands on his time, was kind enough

v

to concern himself meticulously with the finished manuscript, and give me the incalculable benefit of his advice and suggestions.

I would especially thank Lady Eva Dugdale for her courtesy and charm. I have greatly to thank Lady Mount Stephen, Lady Mary Trefusis, Mr. Harry Verney, C.V.O. (Her Majesty's Private Secretary), and Lady Joan Verney.

I am also indebted to the Dowager Countess of Airlie, Dr. Marion Phillips (Chief Woman Officer of the Labour Party), Lady Bertha Dawkins, Miss Violet Markham, Miss Margaret Bondfield, Mrs. Clynes, Miss Gertrude Tuckwell, the late Colonel Frank Dugdale, C.V.O., and Lady Wyndham.

My thanks are due also to Miss Ishbel MacDonald, Miss Lilian Barker, the Marchioness of Londonderry, Mildred Duncan Miles, Lady Ampthill, Sir Robert Baden Powell, Dame Florence Leach, the Dowager Lady Roxburgh, Mrs. St. John Oliver, Mr. G. E. Miles, O.B.E. (late Inspector of the Castle, Windsor), and the Editor of *The Times* for his courteous permission in allowing me to use *The Times* library.

Sir Charles Kenderdine, K.B.E. (Hon. Secretary and Treasurer of Queen Mary's, Roehampton, Hospital), and Major Raphael Jackson (Secretary of Queen Mary's Hospital for the East End), Miss Edith Manning, O.B.E. (late Secretary of Queen Mary's Maternity Home, Hampsted), each rendered me immediate and valuable help.

I regret that I cannot name those, and so thank them, who serve the Great Lady hourly and every day at Buckingham Palace, Balmoral, Sandringham, and

Windsor, and count their service so far back over the years. They gave the rarest help. I thank them.

KATHLEEN WOODWARD.

3 PLOWDEN BUILDINGS,
   TEMPLE.
      February 1926.

ILLUSTRATIONS

QUEEN MARY OF ENGLAND

"REMEMBER THAT LIFE IS MADE UP OF
LOYALTY: LOYALTY TO YOUR FRIENDS;
LOYALTY TO THINGS BEAUTIFUL AND
GOOD; LOYALTY TO THE COUNTRY IN
WHICH YOU LIVE; LOYALTY TO YOUR KING;
AND ABOVE ALL, FOR THIS HOLDS ALL
OTHER LOYALTIES TOGETHER, LOYALTY
TO GOD."

QUEEN MARY, *Buckingham Palace, March 23rd, 1923.*

QUEEN MARY
of ENGLAND

A LIFE AND INTIMATE STUDY

I

THIS is the story of Queen Mary: how Mary the woman made Queen Mary. It is her one enduring romance: this supreme service to her country, to her King, and to her children also—a romance that reads best in the clear light of day. It is an unusual story, being entirely modern and, for the most part, without sensations. So much of sheer character goes to make this romance; and character lately is out of fashion.

Again, that aloofness from the world outside of courts, that unawareness of the practical difficulties and problems which beset the way of those not surrounded by the etiquette and formalities of exalted rank—that "delightful stupidity inseparable from royalty," as it has been called—is conspicuously absent from the point of view and in consequence from the story of Queen Mary. It was this observation which at the beginning so bewildered those who intimately served the new royal mistress when she first came to Buckingham Palace. She lacked that obliviousness to everyday realities which they considered a not unpleasing attribute of royalty, belief in which is with us, too, who are remote from courts, a sort of tradition confirmed by the history of nearly all the Georgian consorts.

It is consoling to know, however, that even those who served her were "two months and more" before they could make up their minds whether it was altogether seemly, quite regal, not a little suggestive of the plebeian, for a queen to be so disconcertingly intelligent as Queen Mary, to care so much about what it did not seem proper for a queen even to know.

When in the "titular and cherished head of the womanhood of England," as Lord Rosebery defined queenship at the opening of Bedford College, one finds in place of that "delightful stupidity," intelligence, goodness, and magnanimity, controlled by rare character, actuated by a passionate love of country, one is moved to say with the tradeswoman in the servants' hall at Buckingham Palace, who was pondering the fraternization of royalty with Labour:

"Dear, dear! All I can say is, who would have thought it!"

It is easy to understand the protest of the two Labour women who worked with Queen Mary during the War on the Central Committee, a protest couched, curiously enough, in almost the same words as those used to me at another time by a lady-in-waiting:

"If only she were not a Queen!"

Then indeed it would be so much easier to write her story.

The career of the Queen is to the overwhelming number of her subjects a closed book which cannot be

read except by those who have reached the woman—
no easy matter; for, added to the restraints of her high
office, there is in Queen Mary a natural reserve which
holds off the forward and precipitate, and a modesty
which altogether disarms the sycophant, but does not
make for revelation.

There is no woman in the British Empire who more
truly shrinks from display and the trumpet-blast.
Born as she was on English soil, bred in its noblest
traditions, in no way is she more English than in her
reserve—in her positive, proud horror of the lime-
light.

"I am English, and I feel it here," said Queen
Mary's mother, the Duchess of Teck, one day as she
slipped off her garden swing, slapped her chest vigorously with all the passionate conviction of five, and
turned to survey the effect of this pronouncement on
her friend. (The late Mrs. Dalrymple often recalled
the incident.) One may be confident, however, that
such a story could not be told of her daughter, Queen
Mary, even at the age of five.

Queen Mary always works unobtrusively and has
thus pursued her royal career. Little is definitely
known about her compared with the much that is instinctively divined!

There is nothing on the surface; so often people are
surprised into knowing her. Miss Ishbel MacDonald
could resolve for me, out of the confusion of impressions that remained from her visit to Windsor Castle
during the premiership of her father, only one or two
clear conclusions: that it is "not easy to know" Queen
Mary. . . . We suddenly realised that one gets to

know her rather through the women of her Court, whose charm, courtesy, kindness, and helpfulness we found inexpressible. They but reflect the Queen. We felt that such women would not be there were the Queen other than she is. . . ." A deduction more than enthusiastically supported by Mrs. Clynes, who visited Windsor Castle during the War while her husband was Food Controller.

It should be added, however, that these women of her Court are the very last people in the world to commit themselves to any verbal eloquence on the subject of Queen Mary: their testimony is felt rather than spoken; and silence in these matters is most acceptable in the inner circle of the royal household. It is a sort of unwritten law, set down by Their Majesties; and curious situations arise when someone generously blunders forward with a bouquet, like the guest recently staying at York Cottage who "seemed to find it difficult to conceal his elation at being there."

One evening, in the middle of a game of bridge, he threw up his hands, and exclaimed:

"Oh, isn't the King a wonderful man!"

The reply came from Sir Charles Cust, the King's oldest equerry and close friend:

"Spades lead. Your turn."

.   .   .   .

"Certainly Fame," cried Bacon, "is like a river that beareth up things light and swoln and drowns things weighty and solid"—a saying applicable to the service of Queen Mary to her country, only a fraction of which is seen and known by the subjects of King

George; that minute part, in fact, which least reveals her mettle and worth. To-day it is a bazaar she opens; yesterday it was the wing of some hospital. To-morrow, perhaps, she will accompany the King to lay the foundation-stone of a great industry, or appear at some historic commemoration. Beyond the formal announcement, set in the well-known phrases, we know nothing.

Yet it is these prescribed duties which bring her to the public eye—that merciless tribunal which rarely errs on the side of excessive charity.

Who knows of her real service in the royal homes? Of the years of assiduous study, the sheer resolution she applied in preparing herself to be the custodian that she is of the treasures of a great Empire?

Who tells of her humanity—the tender heart of the woman allied to the keen intellect that is hers? Of her courage—of her vision—of the passion of her patriotism—her incredible capacity for caring about everything that concerns the Empire—her continued service to and glory in the land of her birth?

"She is so kind, so patient, so balanced, so understanding," said Lord Stamfordham; and I shall not forget the words of one who had served the Queen with the best days of her youth—who had sorrowed and rejoiced with her great lady:

"If ever I were on the eve of some decision that would affect me or my children," she said, "if ever I were in difficulty or distress of any kind, of all women in the world I would go straight to Queen Mary."

She pretends nothing; she is too veracious and candid. There is no smile when it does not come straight and spontaneously; for which reason it is, no doubt, that her smile is so full of charm. She has the unerring sense of atmosphere which belongs to the simple and ingenuous. The warmth of her receptions in the East End of London moves her easily to tears of gratitude; as did her reception in Ireland, soon after her marriage.

It is not only her reserve that hides Queen Mary from public view, but the strength of her personality, the depth of her character, her vast store of practical knowledge and the masculine balance of her intellect. This was felt in her own household long before it silently impressed itself on the world outside; once it disconcerted the curator of a London Museum, who begged that he might answer the questions of his royal visitor afterwards—on paper. It was that same practical intelligence, informed whenever possible at first hand, supplemented by much reading, which exercised various municipal authorities in the region of Bethnal Green, where Her Majesty recently visited some of the "most desolate houses I have ever seen," and made astringent, penetrating comments.

Queen Mary's knowledge and judgment go hand in hand with utter devotion to her husband. Intensive training, added to a natural disposition to withdraw into the shadow, has made her consummate in the art of self-effacement.

Who tells of her reverence for people who do things?

"How well I remember the occasion when a Polish poet was coming to visit at White Lodge," Lady Mount-Stephen once told me. " 'Bricka' (Princess May's governess) must bring out all her books remotely bearing on Polish poets, and her experience of them, if any, in the past.

"Really, it was only Princess May who believed that one could not well meet a Polish poet without at least a tentative grounding in Poles and Polish poetry. I am sure the thought never occurred to anyone else, as I am certain that whatever we got from that particular encounter with the Polish poet, we promptly forgot. Not so Princess May. She could never be found wanting by any Polish poet she might meet in the future!"

.   .   .   .   .   .

Queen Mary commands respect and affection from those whose efforts are devoted, directly and indirectly, to abolishing the very institution she represents; they bow to the woman who would not bow to the Queen.

Consider these two separate testimonies which came unasked from two famous women in the Labour Party —one living, one dead:

"Not a word from me about Queen Mary. It would put the 'Cause' back twenty years!"

And from the greater, now passed away:

"I think the desire of my life is to reveal to the Labour Party the woman that is Queen Mary."

M. Condurier de Chassaigne, in his eulogy of Her Majesty, "the most cultivated woman in the British Empire," during Their Majesties' visit to France before the War, marked also the "noble simplicity of her life," which "contains nothing whereon one can found a sensational story."

Which is altogether true, but for the story of her career. And sometimes, rarely, the shy girl at White

Lodge, then Princess May, would commit herself on this very subject in a letter to a friend: the subject of her future, her career, at a time when even to contemplate a career was still to run the risk of the opprobrious epithet used by Horace Walpole in relation to Mary Wollstonecraft—a "hyena in petticoats."

"I am studying this;" "I am reading" the other. And again: "I am thinking, thinking hard," about something else. "It seems to me so important."

There is a seemliness in the fact that when, in 1914, the call came to women, their "cherished and titular head" should have been Queen Mary at Buckingham Palace, who, watching from afar the gradual emancipation of woman, had yet seized hold on every opportunity which had come with that freedom, so that she was more than ready to assume at a moment's notice no merely nominal but a genuine leadership of the women of the British Empire.

The very fact of Queen Mary's career forms yet another bond to unite her with British women of this generation, and unique as her career is, in essence it is extraordinarily representative. Queen Mary had great opportunities and as great limitations both within and outside of herself. She embraced her opportunities and faced her limitations with the same spirit and energy, in the same passion of service to her country and to her sex, as any distinguished woman pioneer of the times. All of which befits one whose rank is "highest of wives, highest of mothers in her husband's dominion."

Consider, for example, the personal limitations imposed on her by her tremendous shyness, which so greatly embarrassed her during the early years of her life. In the unhesitating opinion of those who know Queen Mary best, "She herself never knew how shy she was, nor how much she suffered from that shyness— and those, too, who had to combat it." The point is, however, as Lady Mount-Stephen well observed to me, her shyness, "acute as it was, never prevented her from DOING anything that came to be done. Such a luxury she would never, for a moment, have considered indulging." Yet it is worth reflecting on the handicap this one quality alone might have been to one who must walk a royal way.

The spirit in which Queen Mary dealt with her shyness, as with any other limitation she might have discovered, is illumined, I think, by an incident which occurred recently in a hospital for sailors disfigured in the War.

Queen Mary was visiting the hospital, which had for its worst patient a sailor with almost the whole front of his face burnt away. Only to see the man was an ordeal even to the members of the staff; and so great was his consciousness of the horror of his appearance that the patient had lost all his confidence.

By the head of the hospital Her Majesty was approached thus:

"We think that if you could possibly sit and talk with him for a while without betraying any conscious-ness of his appearance, it would do him more good than anything else in the world. . . ."

Queen Mary, it should be known, has more than an ordinary natural shrinking and horror from the sight of illness and human mutilation.

For a long time the Queen sat alone talking with the patient in his room, "looking straight into his face, sitting near enough to touch him."

The significance of the story and its relation to the whole of Queen Mary's royal career is in her after-thought:

"It was indescribable. I thought I could not do it; but then, of course, there simply is nothing one can't do. . . ."

II

OF Queen Mary's mother, Princess Mary Adelaide, Duchess of Teck, we know much that is interesting, much that is illuminating of her own personal life and absorbing occupations, the life of her family, the activities of her times and numerous royal connections, and the upbringing of her four children, the eldest of whom, Princess May, was destined to become Queen Mary of England; for the Duchess attended most faithfully to her diary from the year 1853, when she was a girl of twenty.

Before it was published, under the able editorship of Sir Clement Kinloch-Cooke, the diary was scrupulously censored by her children, among others; and many of Her Royal Highness's impetuous summaries and piquant sallies were deleted in the interests of personalities still living, or out of concern for their descendants.

The diary presents an active and vivid woman intensely absorbed in her home, her husband, and her children, not rich enough to delegate to servants and governesses the bulk of her lesser responsibilities towards her home or her children, or desiring to do so, delighting in the social life and the duties incumbent on one so variously connected with the royal families in Europe. When her children were grown up, we see her encouraging the great silk industries of this country, animating philanthropic and charitable organ-

isations, and in a thousand different ways leaving the
sign of her multifarious interests and large bounty,
especially in Kew, Richmond, Sheen, and the district
of Kensington, where she lived during most of her
early married life.

No censorship could efface the essential personality
from the pages of this diary. It "went out" eagerly
to meet all with whom Her Royal Highness came into
contact, and invariably people abandoned themselves
utterly to this uncurbed, extravagant humanity. She
could not pass a child at the stiffest of official functions
without administering a hurricane embrace to the "dear
little tot"; nor could she pass an old woman struggling
along the country lanes of Richmond with her bundle
of sticks without sharing the load.

She gravitated naturally to the laughter and colour
of life and infused them into all her benevolences,
official and unofficial. Her friends adored her and
"more fragrant and less fleeting than the flowers on
her grave was the love and gratitude of the thousands
who mourned her." Her friends were legion; her
Royal Highness had always moved in a large, varied,
cosmopolitan circle who foregathered every Sunday
evening at White Lodge.

Her daughter was passionately attached to her;
Queen Mary's grief at the death of her mother was
the first great grief of her life—overwhelming. To her,
"Mama" had always represented something entirely
and altogether different—someone to whom the difficulties and obstacles which life seemed continually to
present to her not only did not exist, but were often
incomprehensible. "Mama" smiled through the most

"too too impossible" situations, which would have petrified her daughter. Who did not recall the occasion when Her Royal Highness arrived one hour late at a meeting of which she was chairman to find the meeting at a close and rows of anxious faces wondering how on earth the belated chairman would discharge her embarrassment. Then the beautiful voice breaking the silence: "I know that I am a naughty girl; but please don't stand me in the corner!" and, there was no denying, this effrontery usually succeeded.

It is not an extravagance to say that the Duchess of Teck was the most popular royal personage of her time. How the "public" sought her out! And here was no shrinking. She was never sated by the "acclamation of the people." That a crowd should thrill at her approach was to her a source of inexhaustible thrills. To the end of her days she kept this simple, insatiable delight in her popularity.

At the celebration of Queen Victoria's Jubilee, the Duchess of Teck made her first public appearance after her first severe illness. With that precision for place and precedence which obtained strictly in all the royal processions in Queen Victoria's reign, Her Royal Highness was seated very inconspicuously in the glittering assemblage which proceeded to Westminster Abbey, with "her back to the horses." Her delight at being "found" from this extremely adverse view, and the thunder of applause that greeted her, reduced her to an ecstasy of joy. "Even though I had my back to the horses, they found me out!" she said to Lady Mount-Stephen for the hundredth time that day.

The Duchess was the predominant if not the shaping

influence in the life of Queen Mary, from her birth in
Kensington Palace on May 27th, 1867; and in any
attempt to portray the girlhood of the Queen, or to
suggest the influences that surrounded her at that time,
some preliminary sketch of the Duchess of Teck, her
mother, is very necessary.

Princess Mary Adelaide was the youngest daughter
of the Duke of Cambridge, the youngest son of George
III, who in 1817 married Princess Augusta, youngest
daughter of the Landgrave Frederick of Hesse and of
Princess Caroline of Nassau-Usingen. She was born
at Hanover in 1833. The family soon removed from
Hanover to Kew, which was in those days simply a
country village.

To his youngest son, the Duke of Cambridge,
George III bequeathed one of the small properties he
had acquired during his frequent residences at Kew on
the south side of Kew Green, which became known as
Cambridge Cottage.

The Queen's descent from the Cambridge family on
her mother's side is interesting. As a dukedom, the
Cambridge title was first bestowed upon each of the
four children of James, Duke of York, afterwards
James II; but they all died in infancy, and it remained
in abeyance until bestowed by Queen Anne upon
George Augustus, Prince Electoral of Hanover. When
the Prince came to the throne as George II, the dukedom merged in the crown, and was not again revived
until Adolphus Frederick, grandfather of Queen Mary
and youngest son of George III, was created Duke of
Cambridge.

The Queen's mother was always full of stories of her

own childhood at Cambridge Cottage, as indeed she overflowed with entertaining reminiscences of every other period of her life. Always her conversation was abundant and full. One of her famous childhood stories concerned a certain bonnet which the Queen Dowager presented to her when she was a child of five. Queen Adelaide, it seems, had bought it for her own wear, but, finding it unsuitable, passed it on to the child. It was a tremendous creation, covered with feathers; and this bonnet the unhappy child was compelled to wear. Most vividly she recalled, to the end of her days, the agony of being driven from Cambridge House, Piccadilly, to Marlborough House, where Queen Adelaide then resided, in order to show how she looked in the feathered bonnet. Neither her tears nor her entreaties nor her vigorous protestations availed to remove the offensive millinery, which she was most justly convinced did not at all become her five years.

She was a spirited, lively child; her upbringing in "dear little Kew," as she would call it, a quiet, simple matter. Mrs. Dalrymple, who, as a child, played with her, has left one or two excellent pen-portraits of the Queen's mother in her childhood.

"I can distinctly recall the occasion and the appearance of the little Princess, then barely six years old. She was seated in a wickerwork chair, her long fair hair falling in ringlets over her shoulders. The refined features were beautifully moulded, the blue eyes full of expression. . . . We were children together in our games and sympathies. . . . She delighted in discussing certain characters in history, and one day, brandish-

ing a long ruler in her hand, she turned round suddenly
and said to me, 'Can it be possible that when I go to
heaven I shall meet that murderer Henry the Eighth?
Never! I can't believe it! Such a bad character!' "

It was at about this time when a lady, coming to
consult her mother, the Duchess of Cambridge, on
some parochial matter, found the child running round
and round the flower-beds at top speed. "Why are
you running so fast?" "It's the etiquette," panted
the child; "I'm getting rid of it. We've just had a
visit from the Emperor of . . ."

This delightful child grew up into a kind and expansive woman, mother of the future Queen Mary; and
to the end of her life she abounded in that swift
geniality which never fails to capture the "popular
heart." She figured prominently in all "royal" appearances, being the only English Princess of age at
the Court, and the emissary of Queen Victoria, her
cousin, in many philanthropic undertakings that would,
in the ordinary course, have devolved on the Queen
herself.

Always as a girl she was charming, sympathetic,
eager. Lady Caroline Cust said of her, when she was
nineteen: "She was strikingly handsome, and her
beautiful hair and dark blue eyes were much admired.
She was dignified and graceful in her movements and
a remarkably light dancer. . . . She was passionately
fond of music, and sang with great feeling, possessing
a beautiful mezzo-soprano voice. . . ."

After the heat and triumphs of the London season,
Princess Mary of Cambridge would return with her
mother to Cambridge Cottage and "dear little Kew"—

to the orchards and white blossoms, the gathering of primroses in Coombe Woods, and to the song of the nightingale. She appeared in amateur theatricals and even committed herself to verse. There is still extant her "Ode to Lady Marian Alford."

Her letters move with a marked facility of expression, instinct in their frequent italicisms and choice of language with her abundant feeling and emotion— passionate, emphatic, and, when the occasion required, dramatic. A record in her diary, dated December 15th, 1861, from Cambridge Cottage, illustrates her sense of the dramatic and her power to convey it. It relates to the death of the Prince Consort.

"A greyish day and a wretched one! At 8.30 I received the terrible tidings communicated by a telegram from Phipps to Mama, that poor dear Albert had breathed his last shortly before eleven o'clock on the preceding night. The poor unhappy Queen! How will she ever bear it? And those poor people to whom he was Everything! God help them! I hastened to Mama, who, like myself, was quite stunned by the shock and could not find relief in tears, then dressed and went down to breakfast. Little did we dream last night with all our fears of the terrible scene that was just then passing at Windsor! And that HE who had been the ruling head, the very life of that family and household, and the idol of our poor beloved Queen, had gone to his long rest! At two o'clock I left with Geraldine and the Colonel for the Richmond station en route for Windsor, where we arrived just before three o'clock. We walked up the Hundred Steps to the Castle, which, with all its blinds drawn down, looked dreary and dismal indeed. I went in at the Lancaster Tower entrance and in the corridor met Marie Leiningen and Victor Hohenlohe; a little way farther down we came upon poor Alice, Helena, Louise, and Arthur, who all broke down at sight of me, though they strove to regain composure, and to remain as calm as possible for their widowed mother's sake. Alice hurried me to the poor Queen's door, in the hope she would see me, but came out again with the message—'She had not the heart to see me—that day.' We therefore returned to the corridor, where I found Wales with Leiningen and the Duc de Nemours. After Alice had exchanged a few words with the Duc, he took his leave and we all went out for a while, and met little Beatrice and Thurston, who joined us. . . . Wales presently joined us and took me later to see poor dear Albert. He lay on a small bed in the BLUE room (of late years Mama's bedroom), a wreath of white flowers at the head and single ones laid on his breast and scattered on the white coverlid. With a bursting heart I gazed on those handsome features, more beautiful far than in life, on which death had set so soft a seal that it seemed almost as if he were sleeping, and looked my TEARFUL LAST on them! The eyelids were scarcely closed, and there was a smile on the lips which, I like to think, told (as I fondly hoped and prayed it might) of HAPPINESS BEYOND THE GRAVE. I would have given much to be able to kneel down by the bedside, but there were men in the room. . . ."

Early in March 1866 she met her future husband, Prince Teck, at a dinner given by the Duchess of Cambridge at St. James's Place to the Duc and Duchesse d'Aumale.

"The wooing was but a short affair," she wrote to a friend. "Francis only arrived in England on March 6th and we met for the first time on the 7th at St. James's. One month's acquaintance settled the question, and on April 6th he proposed in KEW GARDENS and was accepted."

The bridegroom-elect, Queen Mary's father, was the only son of Duke Alexander of Würtemburg. He was, I have been told, "tall, most handsome, of a commanding presence, amazingly impressive to look at."

III

QUEEN MARY is as proud of her ancestry as the proudest in her realm, and a great authority on the subject. It is characteristic that, finding no authentic or adequate genealogical account of her Teck ancestry, she should, as she did, herself draw it up, presenting a copy to the Royal College of Heralds; a second to her first-born son, the Prince of Wales; and another to Lady Mary Trefusis, who shared the labours of research, which extended over a period of three years.

Her Majesty has a strong, jealous feeling for the Past allied curiously to an unusual capacity for glorying in any achievement of the Present, for the achievements of mind—character—grit. Rufford Abbey, Woburn Abbey—beloved places of her girlhood—may hold her enthralled, humbly reverent in the spell of a great and glorious Past. Her capacity for reverence is inexhaustible. At the coronation of King Edward most people present in Westminster Abbey remarked the regal bearing and intense expression on the face of Queen Mary, then H.R.H. Princess of Wales. After the ceremony a friend asked her:

"What were you thinking in the Abbey?"

She replied: "What it all meant—of the Past."

Illustrious as is Queen Mary's birth on her mother's side—her descent from George III, her great-grandfather, a descent which, if remotely, put her in line for succession to the throne of England (King George and Queen Mary are second cousins once removed)—her forbears on her father's side, through his mother, the Comtesse de Rhedey, are older than the Guelphs, one of the oldest to be found in the *Almanach de Gotha.*

Queen Mary's father, through his mother, was a direct descendant of the historic House of Aba and the royal Arpad Dynasty—a dynasty that was one of the oldest and mightiest in Europe, whose rulers were held in awe by the Byzantine and German Empires. Like France, Spain, and Italy, the Byzantine and German Empires were all tributary to the House of Aba in the early part of the tenth century.

The Queen's father, Count Hohenstein, afterwards Prince of Teck, was born at Vienna on August 27th, 1837. He was the only son of Duke Alexander of Würtemburg, who had married Claudine, Comtesse de Rhedey, no whom, after her marriage, the King of Würtemberg conferred the title of Comtesse de Hohenstein.

It was a romantic marriage, brief and tragic; for about four years after the marriage the Comtesse was trampled to death by a squadron of cavalry, among which she had been thrown by her runaway horse, during some military manœuvres.

The only son of the Comtesse, who was to be the father of Queen Mary, so pathetically bereft of his mother, was brought up in Vienna, and entered the Austrian Army, serving as a lieutenant in the Imperial Gendarmerie Guards. What the boy had lost by the tragically short life of his mother was more than made up for by his marriage to Princess Mary Adelaide of Cambridge; for the Duchess bestowed guidance as well as love on the handsome young officer who wooed her at Kew, and there married her in a rural setting, after a short and romantic courtship.

Abruptly terminated as was the life of the Comtesse, the Queen's grandmother, yet to her son she transmitted abiding traits of her own character and not a little of the artistic sensibilities and talents which distinguished the Queen's father throughout his life; for over and above the Duke of Teck's soldierly virtues, he had a fine natural talent for music and drawing—a talent which, in another sphere, would certainly have stood him in good stead.

To her granddaughter, destined to be Queen Consort of England, the Comtesse bequeathed much of her artistic talent and appreciation. This heritage, forced by the circumstances of royalty to work in a confined medium to utilitarian ends rather than to the end of "Art for art's sake," no doubt explains why Queen Mary is such an excellent connoisseur of art. Her rich, precise, and varied knowledge of works of art, leavened by an acute appreciation of beauty, has served her well in her custodianship of the art treasures and possessions of the royal palaces.

To her granddaughter, Queen Mary, the Comtesse also bequeathed a passion for colour, a passion intense and persistent enough to disconcert the grandchild until she made the illuminating discovery one day that "It must be my Hungarian blood!" To which inheritance, to this day, Her Majesty attributes her almost physical need for colour.

A lady near to the Queen, one who assists no little in the matter of Her Majesty's dress, once told me: "As far back as I can remember, the Queen had loved colours. Curiously enough, long before there was talk of the influence of colour on the mind and body, long before the psychologists formulated and systematised their theories of the psychological effects of colour, the Queen would say: 'I don't know why it is, and it makes me wonder, but actually I do feel different in certain colours! They affect my moods! Really, I do feel different about them!'"

So Queen Mary would reiterate, almost apologetically, to the sceptics about her, who would perhaps have chosen for her other colours and shades. All this long before psychology has more or less sanctioned what were once regarded as their royal mistress's whims.

It is interesting to reflect what a lasting impression seems to have been made on the Princess May when, years ago, in the gardens of "dear little Kew," under the elms at Richmond, or among the primroses in Coombe Woods, she heard the story of her grandmother, the Comtesse de Rhedey—the story of her romantic marriage and tragic death. It is revealing, too, this picture of the shy, quiet, suppressed little English girl, who was to grow up into so deeply reserved and seemingly unemotional a woman, so gripped by the imagination of her romantic grandmother.

What a day it was when to her mother, Princess Mary of Teck, came the wonderful earrings which had belonged to her romantic ancestress—had been actually worn by her grandmother, in those far-off and fugitive Hungarian days!

Again and again the story of the two colossal pearls which compose the Rhedey earrings was reconstructed for her avid ears: how it was said that her ancestress doubted the possibility of their being genuine pearls on account of their unparalleled size, and how her husband drew his sword one day and, in a mighty fit of pique at the doubt cast on his gift, cut one of the pearls apart with one sweep of his sword to prove their genuineness.

To this day the one earring bears the mark of his militant test—there is still the line, faintly discernible, where it was rejoined. Sometimes, on great occasions, these magnificent pearl earrings were worn by the Queen's mother.

In the possession of Queen Mary and her brothers are many treasured relics of their Rhedey ancestry, which had belonged to Ferencz Rhedey, one of the Comtesse's forbears who had played a distinguished part in the history of his country. There is a portrait of Ferencz, and a number of swords and pistols presented to him by the Sultan of Turkey.

In Queen Mary's boudoir at Buckingham Palace is a painting of the beautiful Comtesse; and those who see it are instantly struck by the resemblance, in the sloping shoulders, to Queen Mary.

Of the tangible expressions of Her Majesty's regard for the romantic and fated ancestress must be mentioned a memorial tablet that may be seen in the church of Erde Szent Gyorgy, erected by Queen Mary, when she was Princess of Wales. It reads: "In memory of Claudine, Countess Rhedey, Countess Hohenstein, wife of H.R.H. Alexander, Duke of Würtemburg. Died

1841. Erected by her granddaughter, Victoria Mary, Princess of Wales."

It is a temptation to dwell on the Rhedey side of the Queen's ancestry, her "Hungarian blood"; but I must content myself with a few general facts drawn from accredited Hungarian historians, ancient and modern, about the House of Arpad, from which the Rhedeys can trace their descent.

It supplied some of the most illustrious monarchs in the mediæval world: St. Stephen, Samu, Alba; St. Ladislaus and Kalman—all great kings, whose fame was, from time to time, spread over the civilised globe. The House of Guelph was the first to seek alliance with the House of Arpad—long before it became connected with England. One of the greatest princesses in the history of Christianity, Elizabeth of Hungary, was of the House of Arpad, an ancestress of Queen Mary. Also St. Margaret, who sat on the throne of Scotland, who, too, first saw the light of day in Hungary and in the lustre of close connection with the House of Arpad.

The progenitor of this historic family of Rhedey was one Duke Ede, one of the seven dukes who accompanied his kinsman, Arpad, in his conquest of Hungary more than a thousand years ago.

It would appear that it was a certain Czabanka, living in the year 1199, who was the first to assume the name of Rhedey de Szent Marten, and whose son took a leading part in the reorganisation of Hungary, which, under the rule of the House of Anjou, became one of the most cultured and prosperous States in Europe.

It was at one of the Court balls at Vienna that Prince Alexander of Würtemburg, a young cavalry officer in

the Austrian Hungarian Army, first saw and fell in love
with the enchanting Claudine, Countess Rhedey. They
were married in 1835. The Countess bore a son,
Francis, the Queen's father, and two daughters, Claudia
and Amalia, both of whom bore the title Comtesse of
Hohenstein.

The Countess had only four years of married life
before her sudden and tragic death. She was buried
in the family vault at Erde Szent Gyorgy in Transyl-
vania.

The Queen's paternal ancestry through the House of
Würtemburg descends from the ancient House of
Zahringen, a family closely related to the Guelphs and
the Hohenstaufen Dynasties, who were also the ances-
tors, on the female side, of the founder of the Haps-
burg Dynasty.

The Zahringens had their possessions in the
Duchy of Swabia, the duchy itself being generally
granted by the Emperors of Saxon and Franconian
Houses to their immediate relatives, and from the time
of the Emperor Frederick of Hohenstaufen until that
of Conradin (the last of the line, who was executed in
1268) was held by various members of the imperial
family.

The historic founder of the Würtemburg ruling
house was Ulrich I. He was succeeded by Ulrich II
(1265-1279), whose son, Eberhard the Illustrious,
greatly extended the possessions and power of the
family, and made Stuttgart his capital. With Eberhard V, surnamed "im Bart," the ducal line of Würtemburg commences. This Duke attached to his court
many distinguished scholars of his epoch, and to him

is due the foundation of the famous University of Tübingen in 1477. Frederick I, King of Würtemburg, before he succeeded to the duchy, married, as his first wife, Princess Augusta, daughter of Duke Charles William Ferdinand of Brunswick, and sister of the future Queen Caroline of England; his second wife was Princess Charlotte Matilda, Princess Royal of England, daughter of George III.

The House of Teck was originally founded by Adalbert of Zahringen, who died in 1197; and takes its name from the feudal castle of Teck, situated on one of the many picturesque peaks of Lauter Valley.

Count Hohenstein, Queen Mary's father, was created Prince of Teck by the King of Würtemburg.

There is no doubt that the positive influence in the household at White Lodge, as well as the impetus, emanated from the Queen's mother. She was as full of contradictions as she was full of human kindness; and people, generally, adored her. One of her delicious idiosyncrasies was always and habitually to tear off the unused part of a letter.

"Generous as Princess Mary was," says a friend quoted by Sir Clement Kinloch-Cooke, "it would not be said of her that she was extravagant; while she never refused to give when occasion required, often denying herself to provide for the wants of others, yet in some things she was most careful. Half-sheets of notepaper were always kept; no envelope was destroyed; and every little bit of string was put on one side for further use. In fact, scarcely anything was thrown away."

One is not altogether persuaded, however, that the Duchess was in the habit of practising this extravagant economy. She may have had method with half-sheets of notepaper; but also she had a "chronic habit of giving away just twice as much again as she could well afford." This is the general verdict of the "adorable Duchess" attested to me over and over again.

It is a conviction among those who knew Queen Mary as a girl at White Lodge, and those who were privileged with the friendship of her mother, that, rare and delightful as it was to have so stirring and energetic, so popular, so immensely kind and generous a mother, yet the shy, retiring, and anything but expansive Princess suffered inevitably some eclipse.

The more the Duchess blossomed and extended her large circle of friends, the more her daughter withdrew into her quiet self to play the part of onlooker rather than participator—delighted onlooker though often she was. It was no longer possible to hide herself from people under the folds of her mother's voluminous petticoats, a habit she had as a child, but the tendency was still there.

It was a time of waiting in her mother's shadow; but the waiting period was not wasted. During that time she developed certain qualities, habits, and methods that her mother conspicuously lacked (none knew this better than her mother). Princess May developed, for example, a habit of punctuality—a habit that has grown with the years.

Often the Queen smiles reminiscently over the days at White Lodge when it was not unusual for her to wait an hour or so beyond the time appointed by her mother for dinner. And it must be said that the daughter's experience of the weaknesses of her delightful mother were fully shared by her ladies-in-waiting and others intimately concerned with the Duchess of Teck.

Not long ago, when someone was moved gently to remonstrate with Queen Mary for her distress at the possibility of being two minutes late, "keeping the King waiting for dinner," she said:

"Unpunctuality really distresses me. Ever since I was a girl and saw how inconvenient it made matters for other people, I resolved always to try to be more punctual. Is there anything that sooner ruins good temper than when one is kept waiting, when one is all dressed and ready to start off somewhere?"

And then: "I had so much of it as a girl; that was when I saw what a waste of time and temper it was."

What Queen Mary was not taught by her devoted mother, always so proud of "my Mayflower," at an age which is most susceptible to the claims and feelings of other people, she quietly taught herself. All the large, spacious, humane virtues she acquired from her intensely human mother; she taught herself to economise in time, labour, and energy.

The Duchess had "dash"—her daughter developed an amazing executive faculty. "It was such a blessing, too," I have been told by someone who watched the workings of the affectionate partnership between Queen Mary and her mother. "Really, there was not room in the family for more than one with such 'dash.'"

All of the Duchess of Teck's abounding humanity and kindness are to be found in her daughter; only the expression differs. Confronted with distress, instinctive to both was the immediate impulse, What can I do to help?

Always the Duchess was impelled by that disorderly organ, the heart. More of mind was introduced into her daughter's method. Where the Duchess gathered up her outdoor clothes on the stroke of the moment, dashed to her carriage, and as in a whirlwind approached the scene of the distress, her daughter sat tighter, suffered very much more, and quietly with marked orderliness expressed her sympathy in a very practical fashion, if a much more aloof one.

Mother and daughter were absolutely devoted to each other. Early in her daughter's life the mother understood the acute sensitiveness in her child, and the pain it caused. She saw, with her shrewd knowledge of the world outside, the characteristics and traits in her beloved child that, in a superficial life and among superficial people, were bound to be overlooked.

Soon enough she observed that her daughter had no small talk. She never said what everybody knew about the weather; she was averse from gossip. And what did she do when she met people who could only "talk small"? She simply sat still and said nothing, much to her own evident discomfiture and the discomfiture of her companion. But what to do with a daughter who has no small talk? Only talk more oneself, to make up for the long intervals in the conversation! This the Duchess did remarkably well. Princess May could always do things, and do them better than anyone else. She could talk intelligently, hold with the spell of her mind, and conquer with the charm of her rare smile, the more charming when it came because it was so rare; but when there was nothing to "do," no one intelligent to talk to, and nothing that provoked

Princess May's desperately truthful and captivating smile? This was the Duchess's problem; and unconsciously she seemed to have solved it simply by being the more buoyant, boisterous, and enveloping herself.

Mother and daughter suffered mutually from their shortcomings and excesses; but to all outward appearances they worked amazingly well together. Princess May never did develop the art of small talk and simulation.

IV

THE birthplace of Queen Mary was romantic and auspicious—Kensington Palace, the birthplace of Queen Victoria, her mother's first cousin. Queen Mary was born in the same bedroom as Queen Victoria.

There, too, directly above the bedroom where the baby May was acquainting the whole household with her "fine, powerful lungs" (as her father was quick to observe in his diary), was the famous Council Room of the Palace where in the chill of the early morning, after having been abruptly awakened from her sleep and tumbled out of bed, Queen Victoria in her dressing-gown had received the Archbishop of Canterbury and Lord Conyngham on their knees, to be declared Queen of England.

With many another monarch also was Kensington Palace associated; but all these were eclipsed by her of blessed memory, destined full early to fire the imagination of the Princess May, and always to be the object of her unswerving reverence and veneration.

There came a day when the little girl met her awe-inspiring and venerated relation. On that tremendous occasion Adolphus, the Duchess's next child, "was in the bath, and May terribly shy." "May" distinguished the occasion by dissolving utterly in tears, as was her wont, on meeting far less formidable ladies even than Queen Victoria.

44

Queen Mary's first contacts with the strange new world were made in the rooms at Kensington Palace so imprinted on Queen Victoria's memory—the bedroom where, she was wont to recall, "my earliest recollections were of crawling on a yellow carpet, spread out for that purpose, and being told that if I cried and was naughty, my uncle Sussex would hear me and punish me; for which reason I always screamed when I saw him"; and the nursery, where she developed "a horror of bishops on account of their wigs and aprons. This was partly got over in the case of the then Bishop of Salisbury by his kneeling down and letting me play with his badge of Chancellor of the Order of the Garter."

Nothing at all so fearsome happened to the Princess May, who was carried by adoring arms up and down the corridors where Queen Victoria used to ride on the donkey presented to her by the Duke of York, and look with wondering, if unknowing, eyes at the nursery-books read by her so venerated relation: Mrs. Trimmer's *Steps*, and *Pleasing Tales to Promote Good Manners*.

Apt and fitting historically as was the birthplace of the future Queen Consort of England, domestically it was a very sore trial to her mother. It was a privilege to live in Kensington Palace. The Duchess of Teck was not unmindful of the privilege; but she was also taxed with the insuperable difficulties of making it a home.

Not long before the birth of her first child, Princess May, the Duchess had been given the whole ground-floor of Kensington Palace. It was a gift from Queen

Victoria—a gracious gift, but something of an unmanageable one, and not, perhaps, exactly the place that might have been chosen by a domestically ambitious and exacting newly married woman for her preliminary canters in making a home. However, it was a shelter, and much nearer London than "dear little Kew," to which place the Duke and Duchess had returned from their honeymoon, only to be "snowed up and frozen five days on end, not an omnibus even able to attempt the passage to London," as the Duchess wrote to a friend early in January 1867, four months or so before the Princess May was born.

Love in a cottage at Kew, romantic as it could be during the summer, had its disadvantages in winter, as the Queen's parents testified eloquently during those days; yet icicles from the window-panes and snow barring the doors seem to have left the inner fires notably undimmed. The Queen's parents were a happy couple, living what the Duchess of Teck herself described as a "Darby-and-Joan kind of existence," with all the world before them.

From Kew they had migrated temporarily to 11 Prince's Gate—"a corner house," explained the Duchess, "belonging to my friend Lady Marion Alford." This same letter, dated from Prince's Gate, also reveals something of the quiet domestic life of the Queen's parents at this time.

"We are now beginning life on our own account," wrote the Duchess, "having just completed our small establishment. It is, of course, a great interest and amusement to us both, and you would laugh could you hear me consulting with the steward and lady cook, and giving my orders *bonne maîtresse de maison!* I am thankful to say that the Queen has given us the greater portion of the apartments she and Aunt Kent occupied at Kensington Palace in the days of yore, which the Board of Works promises to get ready for us by the month of May, and which, if they pleased to spend a little money on it, may be made a very charming abode, as the rooms are handsome and comfortable. . . . I am finishing this letter in Francis's sitting-room, whilst he is amusing himself at the piano. I mention this to give you an idea of our *tête-à-tête* evenings, which are very cosy—in the Darby-and-Joan fashion."

The Board of Works were not recklessly extravagant in getting ready the ground-floor of Kensington Palace for the expectant mother; but with that domestic genius which she passed on in abundance to her daughter, the Duchess had completely metamorphosed the somewhat barren rooms on the ground-floor of the Palace. In the new order of things, the Council Room had become an ample and imposing reception-room. The dining-room opened into a salon; and the salon opened into a blue drawing-room. In the room above the blue drawing-room the Princess May was born "on the stroke of midnight," according to the picturesque accounts of the event in the next morning's papers, May 27th, 1867.

There was a devoted and eager company ready to receive the baby: the Grand Duchess of Mecklenburg-Strelitz, the Duchess of Teck's eldest sister, "Aunt Augusta." The Duchesse d'Aumale and Lady Elizabeth Adeane were also present at the accouchement, and as the dawn rose and before it broke over Richmond

Park the Duchesse d'Aumale was speeding to Kew to apprise the Duchess of Cambridge that she was a grandmother.

Queen Victoria was at Balmoral. The news was telegraphed to her with all speed. Before the day was out, one thousand odd visitors had signed their names at Kensington Palace, and left congratulatory messages; by evening, the precise relations of the new-born girl to the two little boys and their sister at Marlborough House were pointedly defined: "A cousin; but not too near a cousin." The prophets had lost no time; and already speculated on the future possibilities of the "English Princess."

The Queen from Balmoral signified her pleasure at the birth; altogether the event inspired an unusual stir and thrill throughout the land and, even at that premature date, a few rays of the "fierce light that beats upon a throne" were, in the popular imagination, refracted over the cradle of the baby Princess at Kensington Palace. Such an "English" Princess!

The world outside was still reverberating from the cannon fire expended on the birthday of Queen Victoria, which had preceded the birth of the Princess May only a few hours.

The augurs seemed all in favour of the new-born Princess in Kensington Palace, except the weather, which was so bitingly cold for May that many gentlemen, for all the momentous events at Balmoral and Kensington Palace, were impelled to notify the Editor of *The Times* that, though it was "but a brief time since we had to record the greatest heat in the shade we had ever observed in May, we have now to remark the greatest degree of cold we ever experienced in May."

Daily bulletins, prominently appended to the Court Circular, were issued from Kensington Palace to acquaint the world outside of the progress of the little Princess and her popular mother. To this news the public faithfully adverted in the intervals of considering two colossal sculptural matters, each of which intimately concerned their Queen and occupied great space in the Press.

One of these matters related to the proposed memorial to the Prince Consort, which now stands opposite the Royal Albert Hall; and the abandonment of the first intention, which was to erect "a vast monolithic obelisk," in favour of a "vast canopy or shrine, overshadowing a colossal statue of the personage to be commemorated, to be enriched throughout with artistic illustrations or allusions to the arts and sciences fostered by the Prince Consort, and the virtues which adorned his character."

The architect's aim, it seems, was to reproduce at full size one of those exquisite jewelled miniatures which the jewellers of the twelfth and thirteenth centuries modelled. This ambition was realised to the satisfaction of Queen Victoria, and now is known as the Albert Memorial.

At Windsor another important piece of sculpture was occupying the Queen's attention, namely, the unveiling of a group of statuary by Mr. William Tweed, representing the Queen and the Prince Consort, which had been placed in the principal corridor at Windsor Castle. It was carved from pure Carrara marble, and, according to *The Times*, the Queen "was pleased to express her entire approval and admiration for it."

The group consisted of life-size figures of the Queen and the Prince Consort, dressed in Saxon costume of the ninth century, "which lent itself favourably to the conditions of sculpture." It represented Queen Victoria wearing a "light and graceful diadem, and a rich mantle"; the Prince Consort also wore a mantle, and in his dress "reminiscences of the antique were favourably discernible. The position of the figures," continued *The Times* correspondent, "readily tells the tale of deep affection and present earthly separation. They stand side by side, Her Majesty looking up at her husband with an expression in which grief and hope are combined, her right hand on his left shoulder, her left hand grasped in his left hand. The Prince is looking down upon the Queen with tender solemnity. . . . On the pedestal is enshrined a line from Goldsmith's 'Deserted Village': 'Allured to brighter worlds, and led the way'!"

The public seems to have turned with relief from these agitating matters, and the controversies they engendered, to the news from Kensington Palace relating to the "English Princess."

Two months later the little girl was baptised by the Archbishop of Canterbury, sponsored by Queen Victoria, the Duchess of Cambridge, the Grand Duchess of Mecklenburg-Strelitz, and the Prince of Wales.

She received the names of Victoria, Mary, Augusta, Louisa, Olga, Pauline, Claudine, Agnes—all of which her mother briskly reduced to "May."

.   .   .   .   .   .

The first year of the Queen's life appears to have been singularly crowded with travel, events, and the society of grown-up people, judging by her mother's diary, which was sedulously posted up during this time. She was barely three months old when she accompanied her parents to Ashridge. The following month the family repaired to Rumpenheim, by way of Paris, where, says the Duchess, "We devoted three days to the Exhibition, to join the family gathering at Rumpenheim, and be present at the funeral of my dear uncle, the Landgrave of Hesse, Mamma's eldest brother. We took our little one with us, and she proved an excellent traveller. Early in October we went on to Stuttgart, to visit Francis's aunt, the Queen Dowager of Würtemburg; and at the end of the month spent a week at Munich, returning home November 12th, to find London all alive with the reassembling of Parliament."

By Christmas, Kensington Palace had been made "fit to receive my belongings," as the Duchess refers to her relations, and, during the Christmas celebrations, "the baby was brought down in its nightgown—a dear, fat, rosy, pretty child," according to Miss Ella Taylor, who seems to have been a constant visitor at the Palace, devoting much epistolary attention to the little Princess.

The baby's path of conquest seems to have been strewn with roses all the way, and, after ravishing all her mother's "belongings" at intervals during the Christmas festivities, the beginning of the New Year was devoted to "grandmamma at Kew," over whom, according to her mother, "May soon made a complete conquest."

Again it is Miss Taylor that limns the little conqueror at Kew. "Such a pet," she wrote, "and will sit for hours on one's knees, playing with her sock, or lying on the floor on a cushion, quite good, requiring no one to dandle or amuse her. How different Princess Mary is to most mothers, who would be so fussy! The Prince quite enjoyed being without the formidable head nurse, so that he could pop into the nursery whenever he liked. One day he undressed the baby and put her to bed. She is very fond of her papa, who looks supremely happy whenever he has sole charge of his little treasure. The other day there was a family group at Kew Gardens and the Duchess fed about sixty ducks to amuse her little granddaughter, who was in the Prince's arms. . . ."

Everywhere and by everybody, the little visitor was surfeited with love and attention. Grandmother at Kew was beside herself with joy; her mother adored her and asked only that she might devote all her attention to her; her father doted on her in the most abandoned fashion, and seems never quite to have sufficiently realised his good fortune. There was only one rift in the lute in that deliriously happy domestic life on the ground-floor at Kensington Palace: the calls of social duties. Thus, to a friend, the Duchess laid bare her soul in the matter, and, incidentally, reveals something of her pride of possession and parentage at this time. The letter is to the Lady Elizabeth Adeane: ". . . There is, however, to me, one drawback attendant upon these country visits, pleasant enough though they be," writes the Duchess, "and that is having to leave my precious child, who is now quite a little companion to her mother. How I do long to show her to you! And how delighted you would be with your 'darling little princess' as you are pleased to call her, and with good right, too. She really is as sweet and engaging a child as you can wish to see; full of life and fun, as playful as a kitten; with the deepest blue eyes imaginable and QUANTITIES of fair hair, a tiny rosebud of a mouth, a lovely complexion (pink and white) and a MOST PERFECT FIGURE. In a word, a model of a baby! You must amiably overlook a mother's fond conceit in her child when reading the foregoing passage, which doubtless is OVERDRAWN, tho' I must say, May wins all hearts by her bright face and smile and pretty, endearing ways. She is wonderfully forward for her age in all things save one, her teeth, at present possessing only two bottom ones, which she cut without any trouble the last week in January; but the top ones are just beginning to show themselves, and I hope will be through soon. I shortcoated her late in autumn, and she looks a perfect picture in her frocks, pinafores, and sashes. Her papa is, in a quiet way, thoroughly devoted to her, and she quite adores him, tho' her mamma is her pet playfellow. . . ."

While the little Princess inside Kensington Palace was content to entertain herself, "requiring no one to dandle her," and incidentally "winning all hearts," the political world of London was speculating over the succession of Disraeli as Prime Minister, Lord Derby having resigned. The Duchess of Teck also was caught up in the excitement. "People wonder and speculate as to whether or no the Disraeli Government will last," she is writing to Lady Elizabeth Adeane. "I confess the new premier in the room of dear Lord Derby seems strange. . . ." Among those who crowded to see "Dizzy," the droll adventurer always incalculable, and invariably comic, and to listen to his parliamentary banter, was the Duchess of Teck; and even in the nursery of her little daughter May could be heard the sounds of the mother's hearty laughter, joining with the rest of the world over the new Prime Minister's gestures in the controversy then raging at Oxford between Science and the Church, which to Disraeli had resolved itself into the one outstanding question: Is man an angel or an ape? To which he made the classic reply: "I, my lord, I am on the side of the angels. . . ."

Disraeli had always been fondly attached to Princess Mary of Cambridge, Queen Mary's mother. "Outside the Queen, and the Prince and Princess of Wales," says Buckle in the sixth volume of his *Life of Disraeli,* "the member of the royal family whom he most highly appreciated, and whom he was most pleased to meet in society, was undoubtedly the vivacious Princess Mary of Cambridge."

The year 1867 passed—the same year that had seen the fall of the Whig Ministry, and Lord Derby called to office a third time; the Oxford Movement; the Fenian Rebellion in Ireland, fed by America and directed by an American "Filibuster" who landed in Ireland to direct the forces of armed rebellion—and the birth of the future Queen Consort of England.

V

IN August a year after the birth of her daughter, the Princess Mary of Teck gave birth to her first son, Prince Adolphus. Prince Francis and Prince Alexander were born later.

The two preceding months had been trying times at Kensington Palace, culminating in a swift and serious illness afflicting "baby May," which to her mother brought such "days and nights of agony as only a mother's heart can fully estimate," as she wrote to her friend, Mrs. Dalrymple; "but I was wonderfully supported through them, and God was pleased in His mercy to spare the little life to us we so TREASURE. For upwards of twenty-four hours it trembled in the balance, and my heart quivered with it; then there came a blessed change, and oh! the feeling of intense relief and deep thankfulness! It was not to be described. . . .

"She was seized on July 18th with sickness, for which proper remedies were at once, and apparently very effectively, applied; for on the Tuesday following, May was out again for half an hour in the cool of the day. Whether she caught a slight chill, or the effluvia from the pond in Kensington Gardens, which was in a very unhealthy state, and which the nursery windows face, affected her, I know not. But that very night she had an alarming relapse, and all the next day lay in a state of collapse. Dr. Farre was called in, and toward evening, thank God, the treatment began to tell upon the child, and the attack to yield to it. From that time she mended steadily, although slowly, and on August 4th her grandmamma very wisely insisted on carrying her off to Kew, to be away from the pond, and out nearly all day in the garden under the shade of the old chestnut-tree."

The Round Pond in Kensington Gardens has undergone rigorous changes since the Queen was a baby at Kensington Palace; for in those days it was dirty and neglected, filled with stagnant water, the effluvia of which were well calculated to breed a fever.

The old Duchess at Kew watched her little charge through convalescence, and, after her mother had returned from a visit to Queen Victoria at Balmoral, toward the end of the year, the Princess May, barely two years old, and her brother Adolphus, a lusty baby in arms, were taken by express command to visit Queen Victoria at Windsor.

It was the first real meeting between godmother and child, and, when Princess May had wept her full flood at the introduction, she settled down to charm the greatest of all her royal relations. She ate with the Queen, rode with the Queen and, finally, passed out from under the inspection with high honours and flying colours, and the unstinted royal approval.

As the child grew up that approval became more marked and affectionate; her *savoir faire*, as Lady Eva Dugdale described it to me, completely engaged Queen Victoria.

The Duchess of Teck at this time seems to have been identified with few matters outside her home and the upbringing of her children. Her diary is redolent of

the quiet life at White Lodge. Such passages as:
"We had our tea on the lawn with all the children";
and "We hid the Easter eggs for May in the corridor
till nearly four, then into the garden with Francis and
May. . . . Sat out writing, playing with the chicks
(the blessed trio) and having tea with May and Dolly,"
constantly recur.

The Marlborough House children were constant
visitors at White Lodge. "April 19th. . . . We sat
in the drawing-room till Mamma arrived, and then
adjourned to the garden, where we found the two
youngest Wales children—Victoria and Maud. . . .
We had tea out of doors, the children having theirs in
the corridor. Lady Alice Peel came, and when she
and Mamma had left, I went in to play with the chicks
in the drawing-room. At six the Waleses departed,
but I stayed with May and Dolly till nearly
seven. . . ."

One of the Princess May's first excursions into the
great outer world was taken in company with her cousins,
when their mother, Queen Alexandra, then Princess of
Wales, took them to the Amphitheatre, Holborn, in
1871, where, as it is most solemnly recorded, the
elephant especially entranced Princess May.

Of all the "blessed trio," as the Duchess called her
children, May, Adolphus, and Francis, Princess May
seems to have been the most exemplary. At her first
attendance at a steeplechase the Duchess notes in her
diary: "May behaved herself most beautifully." Mr.
English, the Kensington butcher, presented the little
girl with a goat and equipage. It rained on the morning of the presentation; but "May" circumvented the

weather by riding the goat-carriage in the corridor and so delighting the two boy "chicks" that "she had her tea with us," as a reward.

The Princess's first social appearance came a few days later, when she accompanied her mother to Hampton Court, and signified her feelings by bursting into tears: "May was shy at first, and then wept," the Duchess records, "but finally recovered herself and played with Daisy and her little sister, and was in tearing spirits all the way home. . . ."

Princess May seems to have been a singularly shy little girl, and her invariable procedure on first meeting new friends and companies was to burst into tears. As the years passed she abandoned this somewhat frank and direct expression of her discomfiture; but the shyness remained to make her quiet and restrained always, except in the company of friends, or wherever she sensed perfect naturalness and composure in the person she met.

It is a shyness of reserve rather than a shyness of self-consciousness, and it has always remained with her. Its outward signs are well known to those whose service is devoted to her, and who are privileged to observe her in a variety of circumstances, meeting that homogeneous stream of persons that royalty is fated to have always with them. There comes a faint, hardly perceptible stiffening of the back, a drawing up as it were of the figure, just the flicker of an enigmatic expression passes over the Queen's face—and those who know, observing these things, know also that the Queen is not at ease. It is a great protective, this shy reserve; and has notably misled many people.

© W. & D. Downey

PRINCESS MAY OF TECK AT 7.

PRINCESS MAY AT 16, WITH HER MOTHER AND BROTHERS

There are many stories of Queen Mary's shyness as a girl, and later, when her life was made up of many social comings and goings. It is a fact that, in spite of her discomfiture on occasions, she never tires of meeting people; indeed the Queen delights in social life.

There is a delightful story told me by Lady Mount-Stephen who (with her aunt, the late Lady Wolverton, a neighbour of the Princess May of Teck at Richmond and one of Her Royal Highness's closest friends) knew Queen Mary as a girl, and has watched her through the years with the eyes of a great love and devotion.

Queen Mary, then Princess of Wales, was staying with Lady Mount-Stephen in Hertfordshire. They were going together to pay a call at Woburn Abbey. Hardly had they started on their way when a manure-cart crashed into the car. The Princess of Wales remained "desperately calm"; Lady Mount-Stephen, in what she described as a "fine frenzy," called down imprecations on the cart driver, and announced her immediate intention of informing the local chief constable of police; for not only was the man stupid, but apparently without a vestige of right to be there.

H.R.H. smiled engagingly and said: "I beg of you not to complain; for then by to-morrow it would be in all the newspapers."

The journey was renewed—Lady Mount-Stephen "hot, flustered, all agog;" the Princess of Wales "horribly calm"—until they came almost to the end of the drive and in sight of Woburn Abbey, when the situation inside the car dramatically changed.

The Princess began to fidget uneasily and look perturbed; Lady Mount-Stephen, having by this time recovered equilibrium, looked wonderingly for the cause of the sudden alteration.

"Oh dear," sighed Her Royal Highness, "I feel so shy. Oh dear; why am I so shy? meeting people. . . ."

Said Lady Mount-Stephen vigorously: "Shy! You shy!" Then, no doubt with memories of her own receiving of royalty in time past, "How do *you* think *they* feel—waiting to receive you! Do you not realise how shy of you *they* must be feeling?"

And with a delicious look of surprise and incredulity, the Princess of Wales said: "You mean you really think that they are shy of *me!*"

"Yes, indeed," said Lady Mount-Stephen grimly.

. . . . . .

Again, by the gift of Queen Victoria, the home of the Duke and Duchess of Teck was removed from Kensington Palace, and the unsalubrious effluvia of the Round Pond, to White Lodge, Richmond Park, where the Princess May grew to girlhood and womanhood, and whence she drove to Buckingham Palace many years later as the bride of Prince George. It is a place that is full of memories of the infinite kindness of her mother, whereon her personality is ineffaceably stamped, and her kind bounty and charity grown almost legendary in its annals.

That there "never has been such times," either before or since those days of the Duchess and her growing family at White Lodge, is the sentiment of the older inhabitants of Richmond who, as children or as young men and women in those days, looked upon the lady up at White Lodge as a never-failing fountain of sympathy, a model of all the wifely and domestic virtues, a constant and vigorous source of practical advice and help; a very embodiment of all English virtues and an incomparable mother to her three little boys and their sister "May."

George II had caused White Lodge to be built for his occasional residence. It was first called Stone Lodge, and later the New Lodge, and in those early days consisted simply of a central block with stone columns supporting the pediment. It is about a quarter of a mile from Spanker's Hill, on the road to East Sheen, surrounded by rich, fragrant, generous, and densely wooded country, easily accessible to and from London, yet having a quietness, a detachment as of the very heart of the country.

White Lodge looks down upon a beautiful avenue of trees, nearly a mile in length—Queen's Ride it is called, from its having been the favourite ride of Queen Caroline, wife of George II. Here the Princess May was brought; and her coming was eloquently described to me by one of the gate-keepers and his wife, now residing in Richmond Park, grown old most gracefully in the service of "the family" at White Lodge. "The Princess, as I remember her," he said, "was a tall, thin little girl, in a short frock, white socks and high-topped boots. She grew up to be very genteel and ladylike."

Here the gate-keeper's wife interposed with a more meticulous and detailed description of the "little Princess." "A pretty child she was, with fair hair, blue eyes—very English-looking," she said. "In her ways,

even as a little girl, she was different to her mother—
quieter-like. And she was what you would call an
inquiring sort of child. Many's the question she asked
me about the flowers and things in the garden that
regular stumped me—questions you wouldn't expect
from a little girl like that.

"I think she must have been interested in flowers and
shrubs; for often I came on her round and about the
way to Coombe Woods, looking solemn-like at some
wild-flower she found by the way. . . .

"She always came in your house quiet-like and made
herself at home. Now the Duchess, too, was homely;
but she sort of swept down on you. And she wouldn't
say anything unusual, or ask about things that other
people didn't ask about. The little girl was different;
and I soon got to know that if I didn't know the right
answer to the question she asked, it was better not to
say anything. Such a one she was for finding out about
everything! . . . And, later, summing up her memory
of the Duchess of Teck:

"She was the kindest lady that ever lived round these
parts, concerned about everyone. She was fond of
giving presents, too—if you ask me I think she always
gave away as much again as she could afford. She was
like that. And up in her own drawing-room she would
have us to give the presents. I remember she gave
me a cloak once. That was fun; for my little boy stood
by looking on so seriously that the Duchess threw the
cloak over him, and he looked so foolish that we all
burst out laughing. . . .

"That was how it was; she left a laugh with everyone she saw."

To this day, many stories are current at Richmond about the comparative state and splendour in which the Queen's parents lived at White Lodge; and these stories are not without a touch of irony. It is true that the Duke and Duchess had each their carriages and horses, and other such evidences of wealth given to them with the gift of the Lodge; but unfortunately they were without the necessary money to maintain such splendour!

It was a minor omission, not known to Richmond, and one that did much to complicate life at White Lodge. It is well known among the friends of the Duchess that the family was, relatively, desperately poor; and the little matter of making both ends meet was quite enough to tax all the ingenuity, the optimism, and the aplomb of the Queen's mother. Royal luxuries were more or less thrust upon them; and their joint finances could only bear the strain of a comfortable private country life.

All this was soon known to the little Princess, and doubtless, too, she was made aware that both she and her brothers owed much of the cost of their education to their grandmother Cambridge at "dear little Kew." It was to Kew and her mother that the Duchess of Teck looked in times of stress and need, and rarely was the source found wanting.

Grandmamma Cambridge adored the children; the children lavished affection on their grandmamma; and in the twilight of her days, cut off from society by illness, a prisoner in St. James's Palace, she reaped the benefits of her generosity a hundredfold; for the children were her constant visitors. Every Sunday and every Christmas they came, with a new hymn or carol to pipe round her invalid couch; and when the invalid could no longer even knit, there were always the "chicks" to think about—to watch them grow, to scheme for, to speculate on their futures.

The Duchess of Teck's own opinion of her growing family she expressed often and with great enthusiasm. Writing to the Hon. Lucy Kerr when the Queen was five, she says: "I am thankful to say that May is once more a strong child, and a tall, wiry one beside her brothers, the younger of whom is a perfect little giant, and a great pet. Dolly and Frank are splendid specimens of boyhood, the one golden-haired, the other chestnut brown.

In another letter, after her third son was born, she is writing: "My little ones are very flourishing, and great darlings. The boys are said to be as handsome as ever, and No. 3 I think bids fair to surpass his brothers! He has splendid dark-brown eyes and is wonderfully like his father, and such a pet! so merry and full of fun and mischief, and all over dimples. . . .

"The trio are getting on nicely with their lessons under the tuition of their daily governesses (each good in her way), and May and Dolly are really making excellent progress.

"May is, I am thankful to say, outgrowing her delicacy, and has greatly improved in looks. She is quick and clever and very musical, and all three promise to be very apt pupils."

VI

THE early girlhood of Queen Mary was quiet, secluded, and generally undistinguishable from the growing-up period of any well-born English girl of the time. Excursions into the world of her own age, outside White Lodge, were few and discriminating; and the attitude of her mother in these matters is summed up in the following extract from a letter she wrote at the time in reply to an invitation for her children.

"Much," wrote the Duchess, "as I should like to comply with your kind request, I fear it is impossible for me to send the children to you to-morrow, as they have been out to children's parties two days running this week, and I fear too much dissipation will have a bad effect on their lessons. Trusting you will forgive and understand my scruples. . . ."

A "nice Hanoverian governess" that was enlisted for her, the society of her mother and father and her three sturdy brothers, her cousins at Marlborough House— Cousin Georgie, Cousin Eddy (the late Duke of Clarence) and their sisters constituted the general company in which she moved, with many visits to Grandmamma Cambridge at Cambridge Cottage.

Describing herself at this time, Queen Mary has said that she was "very naughty, very happy, and very uninteresting." Her mornings were spent at lessons

with the "nice Hanoverian governess." In the afternoons she roamed Sheen or Coombe Woods with her
brothers, or visited with her mother; for Queen Mary
was early broken in to the philanthropic harness. Occasionally, as a girl, she sold at bazaars for charity, and
Miss Violet Markham recalled for me a vision of the
Princess May in her teens, selling at a Richmond bazaar.
There is a story that, as a girl, she was once selling
in a bazaar at Kew Gardens, with her mother and her
cousins Louise, Victoria and Maud of Wales. A lady
bought a fan of Princess May, and asked her to auto-
graph it.

"With pleasure," she said, flushing, "but are you not
mistaking me for one of my cousins of Wales? I am
only May of Teck."

The life at White Lodge was a family life in the
fullest sense of the term; and in the summer evenings,
under the apple-tree in the garden, the family regularly
foregathered before bedtime.

It was a simple creed that the Duchess held with
regard to the growing-up time of her children. She
wished them to be educated; nothing, therefore, was
allowed to interfere with their studies. She wished
them to be strong, healthy children; and the splendid
health of Queen Mary, in the most trying circumstances, is a tribute to her mother's unremitting
attention in her youth.

As a child, Princess May was not strong. Mrs.
Dalrymple reminisces illuminatingly on the distress
that this occasioned the Queen's mother—her deep
"concern during a slight illness of Princess May's, lest
she should grow up delicate," and the "Duchess's firm

resolve that her daughter's girlhood should be absolutely free from excessive gaieties and excitements," and
such like nervous exhaustions.

"A child has enough to do," said the Duchess of
Teck one day to Mrs. Dalrymple, "to learn obedience
and attend her lessons and to GROW, without many
parties and late hours, which take the freshness of
girlhood away, and its brightness and beauty. Then,
children become intolerable. There are too many
grown-up children in the present day!"

The Duchess was more than rewarded for her jealous
watchfulness. Wherever I have been, to whomever I
have spoken about the girlhood and early womanhood
of the Queen, always I hear the same story with the
regularity of a Greek chorus, were my informant some
high lady of the realm, or the lowliest gate-keeper's
wife, who, pushing her perambulator through Richmond Park, espied a vision of the young Princess, flying
on her pony, hair streaming on the wind, down Queen's
Walk. "Such a figure! Fine—full of health, not
athletic in the horsy sense"; but quietly whole.

I shall long remember the fine scorn with which an
old septuagenarian, discoursing to me by the Robin
Hood Gate of Richmond Park on the "superbity" of
the Princess May as a girl, dismissed all modern efforts
on the golf course, and in the gymnasium, to achieve
that grace and splendidness which the Queen, as a girl,
wore with such ease. "The Duke of Teck," he proceeded, "didn't believe in no rough, horse games for
women, he didn't. It wasn't no golf that produced our
Princess."

Queen Mary's father, as a matter of fact, was averse

to any form of sport for women. He had precise notions of the conduct that befitted a lady; it was repug-
nant to him even to see his daughter "in the gardens
without gloves," Lady Mount-Stephen has told me—
prohibitions not, it would seem, unfamiliar to girls of
the time. Queen Mary never did develop a taste for
sport.

Testimony to her capacity for physical endurance
there is no end. It has impressed everyone. "The first
and only glacier I ever negotiated in my life—or ever
will," Lady Wyndham has told me, "was in the company of the Queen, then a girl staying with her parents
at St. Moritz." Relating the thrilling adventure, Lady
Wyndham constantly recurs to Queen Mary's inexhaustible freshness and strength, which, at least on the
glacier, seemed to Lady Wyndham the most enviable
of all gifts of the gods.

"She simply went on and on." The glacier soon
reduced Lady Wyndham to sheer prostration; for a
long time after she craved nothing but rest, being, as
she says, "of cities, not over strong; and entirely unfamiliar with glaciers—knowing absolutely nothing
about them. . . .

"Afterwards I asked Princess May what she did
when she got back to the Hotel Victoria.

" 'Oh, I had a hot bath,' she replied airily, 'and then
it seemed as if nothing had happened!' "

Not the least delightful incident of the day, according to Lady Wyndham, was when she appeared on the
glacier with exceedingly high-heeled shoes—"knowing
nothing about glaciers. . . ."

"We had hardly started," she said, "when all the leather came off the heel—it shone white. . . ."

That elusive dignity of bearing which instantly impresses all who have seen Queen Mary was apparent in her as a girl. Lady Mary Trefusis, who accompanied the Queen on her tour of Australia and later on a visit to France, has told me how that dignity "impressed everyone who caught sight of her.

"I used to love to sit and watch the expression on people's faces when the Queen came into a room," said Lady Mary. "There was nothing self-conscious about her bearing. I am sure that if she had been aware of the sensation her slightest movement created she would have been awfully discomfited. It just happened. She sailed into the room—and everyone held their breath.

"Always it made her the centre of attention. I grew adept at reading the expressions on people's faces when they first beheld her. 'How does she do it?'

"It was as if all her character were in the movements of her body: quiet, superb, instantly impressive. So for as my observation went, it impressed everyone alike. I particularly remember the sensation it created in France, how the Frenchwomen were characteristically frank in their expressions, and would secretly consult one on the art of emulating that inimitable grace and dignity which with the Queen was not the result of training or art, but simply and purely an unconscious expression of character. . . ."

In one way the Fates were wonderfully kind to the sensitive little girl growing up in her quiet, thorough way and meditating much on the scheme of things—in their selection of Richmond and White Lodge, commanding that majestic walk where Jeanie Deans pleaded for the life of her sister with Queen Caroline. There are few places in England more richly endowed with natural beauties and historic associations than Richmond.

Poets, she learned—being then of a greatly inquiring turn of mind, had tuned their songs at Richmond—Wordsworth, and the humbler Thomson, who, in May 1736, had settled there in a small house to complete his "Castle of Indolence," after a gestation of the "Seasons," joined with Malbet to produce the masque of "Alfred," first represented at Cliveden-on-the-Thames before the Prince of Wales.

Yet a greater poet by far than Thomson, she learned, had been associated with the scenes of her girlhood. Shakespeare's plays were repeatedly performed at Richmond before Queen Elizabeth; and in Shakespeare's time, as the "nice Hanoverian governess" would inform her pupil, there were Bardolphs living in the vicinity; and there was actually for them to see, one day on a pilgrimage, an elaborate monument in the parish church to Simon Bardolph.

Painters from abroad, lured by the renown of Richmond, had left a wealth of work to testify to the inspiration it had yielded them—painters of the French, Flemish, the Swiss, and Italian Schools; and one of the earliest paintings extant of Richmond Hill was left by Reynolds, who had settled there with his sisters, bringing Fleet Street in his train in the shape of Johnson, Goldsmith, Burke and Garrick—to disport in the scenery and abundance of rich trees.

There were endless historic associations for the little girl to acquire, with her passion for finding out about things, and the help of the "nice Hanoverian governess."

VII

"GUSSY," as the Duchess of Teck invariably referred to her elder sister, Princess Augusta Caroline, Grand Duchess of Mecklenburg-Strelitz, and "Aunt Augusta" to Princess May, was one of the few appreciable influences in the girlhood and early womanhood of Queen Mary. Aunt Augusta at Strelitz had received regular visits from her niece from the days when she was brought to Germany in long clothes, up to the year immediately preceding the War. More frequently, however, aunt and niece met on the Grand Duchess's frequent visits to the land of her childhood, in "dear little Kew." She had been present in Kensington Palace at the birth of Queen Mary.

The Grand Duchess was one of the most interesting women in the Cambridge line—a woman most passionately and pathetically English in all her interests and her affections. She lived a long life, and died at the age of ninety-three, during the progress of the War, cut off from all her English friends and associations, and unable to see her beloved niece, Queen Mary, in England. She died away from all she loved and with the constant cry on her lips—"*My* country at war with the country of my adoption!" To the end of her long life she retained all her vigour and mental alertness, only to be tortured by an unbridgable separation from her loved ones and to die in the stress of her own sorrow. To the end also, she insisted on being addressed on the envelopes of her letters as "Princess of Great Britain and Ireland."

The Grand Duchess was devoted to her "dear May," and was at no pains to conceal her devotion. Her niece more than reciprocated the affection. Strong links bound the child and woman together—links of mutual affinities and interests, as well as the ties of blood.

From one or two friends of the Queen's girlhood who often accompanied the family at White Lodge on their frequent visits to Strelitz I am indebted for my knowledge of the character and mind of the grand old lady who remained to the end of her days greatly, undividedly, devoted to England and the scenes of her childhood at "dear little Kew."

I give the following picture as it was given to me by Lady Eva Dugdale, one of the many devotees of the Grand Duchess of Mecklenburg-Strelitz. While we talked there was before us a photograph of the Duchess, "one of the last she had taken." It portrayed a rather small and extremely erect lady, dressed in black, with a wealth of white hair, sharp-featured and of medium height, with an intellectual brow and markedly kind eyes. Her mouth showed full and wide, and sensitive to a degree.

"Always her heart was in England," said Lady Eva; "it was pathetic to watch her feeding on every memory, every relic, every association with England."

She read *The Times* every day. It was like a religious observance with her. Other English newspapers, too, she devoured, though not so meticulously perhaps as *The Times*. Often they had to take the English papers away from her.

"There was none so well informed and up-to-date on all matters English as Aunt Augusta—on matters political, social, intellectual, and artistic. To get a sound judgment and perspective of any question of the hour, you had to go to Strelitz, to Aunt Augusta. It was almost a joke with us in those days—the extent, variety, the reach, and the lucidity of her knowledge of what was happening to us in England. Literally, we all sat at her feet, young and old, men and women, politicians and *littérateurs* from England, to learn what was meet to know. None cared as she cared about what was happening in England; as a mother knows every mood and motive in the working of her child's heart, so she knew England. . . ."

Whether they asked her of the past, or whether they asked her of the present, or called upon her to speculate for the future, she was always equal to the request. The mention of a name in passing was enough to set the Grand Duchess off on an enchanting narrative. She was consummate in conversation. When Princess Mary of Teck, the Queen's mother, died, it was the Grand Duchess who took her place—Aunt Augusta that represented always the inspiring link with the past.

To come from England was to come to Strelitz with more than a passport to the abundant kindness and hospitality of the Grand Duchess; it was to bring her a whiff of home—of fragrant Kew, with its white blossoms rioting with primroses, of its fruit-laden trees and wild-flowers positively dancing out of the hedge-rows; and of the garden at Cambridge Cottage under the "dear old chestnut-tree," where, throughout the long, cool evenings of the summer months, she sat with her mother, the Duchess of Cambridge.

In far-away Strelitz her heart was in Kew, and, as the years passed and the ties of separation were strengthened, her "patriotism became one of the passions of her life," Lady Eva Dugdale has assured me.

By all who were privileged to know the Grand Duchess it is testified that she was one of the most intelligent women of her time. Like her sister, the Queen's mother, she had a great need and capacity for human affection. She was unlike her sister, however, in most other characteristics. It is to the Grand Duchess that one must look for many of the mental and personal traits that distinguish her niece, Queen Mary of England.

In her intellectual range and grasp of politics and sociological questions, in the clarity of her views and the eminent soundness of her judgments, above all in her balance, Queen Mary far more strongly resembles her Aunt Augusta than her mother, Princess Mary. Other attributes and qualities niece and aunt shared conspicuously. Common to both was a zest for the acquisition of knowledge, which made the Grand Duchess such a rare, entertaining, and enlightened companion, just as it has made the life of Queen Mary so full, so vivid, and various.

Like her aunt, Queen Mary is never bored when she is left to her own resources. There is always something to learn! The Grand Duchess was an excellent and fluent linguist; and there are those who can remember her sustaining a vivid conversation with four persons in her drawing-room—an Englishman who understood only English; a Frenchman who understood only French; a German and Italian also strictly limited to their native tongues.

How much she infected her niece with her own discovery of the mind's infinite capacity to learn and to be interested, it is hard to tell, though it is for all the Queen's friends to know of the niece's devotion and gratitude to her aunt.

At Strelitz there was always Aunt Augusta, the wise, the good, the kind, the eminently intelligent, the passionately patriotic, the lover of England with whom one could talk over things of import, and things not of import, that were taking place in England. Was it Mr. Gladstone stirring up and dominating the political world with his extraordinarily masterful figure? Aunt Augusta watched all the political convulsions about him, and was precisely versed in the upheavals which followed on his conversion to Home Rule for Ireland.

Did conversation at Strelitz turn upon the Æsthetes, those Bright Young People of the Eighties who attracted the frosty irony of Gilbert and exercised all the pictorial satire of Du Maurier in *Punch?* Aunt Augusta, with her knowledge and acquaintance of the English reviews and magazines, was more than equal to the occasion.

Remote from the exuberances of the Æsthetes were Huxley and the Evolutionists working out the Darwinian theory and rewriting the book of Genesis in modern scientific language. Here was another matter to engage Aunt Augusta's attention and provide material for conversation; and Bradlaugh, at Westminster, a tremendous Titan, dressed like a nonconformist, questioning the Oath of Allegiance in the intervals of being flung out of the House by half a dozen burly policemen.

Mrs. Fawcett and Lady Frances Balfour were sounding the first faint cries of "Votes for Women" that struck so shrilly on the ear of the later Victorians, and drawing up the petition of the "hyenas in petticoats." Florence Nightingale was living in semi-regal seclusion off Park Lane after the strain and ardours of the Crimea, receiving numerous distinguished visitors.

Carlyle, George Eliot, Borrow, Fitzgerald, and Disraeli were British names in letters, and consequently of significance to Aunt Augusta. Morris was pursuing his boisterous Socialist campaign—gusty, intensely preoccupied as ever, singing his songs of "Sigurd" and "Atlanta," and inspiring the Pre-Raphaelite Brotherhood. There was much to say about Morris at Strelitz, as Aunt Augusta turned the variegated pages of his interests in painted glass, Arras tapestry woven with high-warp looms, his carpets, embroideries, tiles, furniture, house decorations, printed cotton goods, paperhangings, upholsteries, not to mention the breathless creations shot out from his Kelmscott Printing Press and his Romances which came out serially in the *Oxford and Cambridge Magazine*—all for the benefit of her visitors from England.

At the Pines, Putney Hill, Swinburne was living the suburban life, a small, great-headed, tripping figure singing his "Songs Before Sunrise" as he high-stepped past the birch-crested heather and gorse ravines over Wimbledon Common and Putney Hill. Meredith was writing *Beauchamp's Career* at Dorking; Burne-Jones, Watts, Millais—whom the Princess May was to know so well later on—were at the summit of their productive power.

When, as often, the Grand Duchess paused to glance at the English Stage, there were Ellen Terry and Irving at the Lyceum as Hamlet and Ophelia, dominating drama; Beerbohm Tree at the Haymarket, and Nellie Farren (Mrs. Soutar) making high cockney comedy at the Gaiety in all the time she could spare from driving her phaeton and pair down Bond Street. Many of these artists frequented her sister's cosmopolitan circle at White Lodge.

Not that the chances of politics in England interested only Aunt Augusta. Her sister, the Duchess of Teck, took a lively interest in the proceedings at Westminster, all of which were reported in due course to Queen Victoria at Balmoral.

The following extracts from the Duchess of Teck's diaries illuminate not only her political interests, but also the heterogeneous celebrities she gathered together at White Lodge:

"*May 30th*, 1882.—I have just returned from the two Houses of Parliament, having been first to the House of Commons to see the Bradlaugh episode, which, though not by any means edifying, was most curious, and had resulted in a grand majority against the Government—a delightful beginning for the session. . . . Bradlaugh spoke very distinctly, and, when not carried away by passion, with studied effect like an actor, his object evidently being to pose as a sort of tribune of the people. The mock humility with

which he began to address the House soon gave way
to rage, and, before he wound up with his grand per-
oration, he had repeatedly shaken his fist at the Oppo-
sition."

"*November* 13*th*, 1881.—Mr. Irving and Miss
Ellen Terry came out to luncheon, at which Irving
was my neighbour. Miss Terry was quite done up,
and rested in the Boudoir with Lady Hopetoun and me,
interesting us much by her outpourings. . . . We were
sixteen at dinner and afterwards told ghost stories till
towards midnight. Then a bear fight, farm-yard performance, and, finally, a grand hubbub *chez moi!*"

It was the deepness and intensity of the Grand
Duchess's political interests that distinguished her from
the Duchess of Teck; but it was neither her political
interests nor her intellectual capacity that most profited
her niece, the future Queen Mary. It was rather her
wisdom, and the experience which had brought the
wisdom.

To others, also, Aunt Augusta extended her counsels
and advice when they were sought in the long winter
evenings at the Castle of Mecklenburg-Strelitz, where
the long corridors had often resounded with the noisy
gambollings and games of "May" and the "Boys" as
they rushed about in a wild, mad chase. "Now and
then," says Miss Friederichs, recalling fondly, "May
would suddenly come to a standstill when the silver
arrow round which was coiled her fair hair had slipped
out, and she would stand enveloped in what looked like
a long cloak of waving gold . . . !"

VIII

TWO considerable influences in the life of Queen Mary during the most impressionable years of her life, when she was growing up, I have already dwelt on. They were, first and foremost, her mother, Princess Mary of Teck; the Grand Duchess of Mecklenburg-Strelitz, her mother's sister, being the second.

There was, however, a third influential person who helped to mould the young girl's life. This was Madame Bricka—"Bricka" to the household at White Lodge, an Alsatian governess-companion selected for the Princess May, in succession to the "nice Hanoverian."

Bricka was very much a personage in the household at White Lodge, wielding her sway over the most malleable years of the Princess with unceasing pride, and an intensity and thoroughness that left nothing wanting. She did more: she left her pupil with a lasting sense of gratitude, a gratitude which, later on, when Bricka was no longer able to work, was expressed in an exceedingly and enduringly practical manner.

Bricka! Her figure seems always hovering, shadowy-like in the background of the Queen's growing years—the vehement, volatile, passionate Bricka, with all the current of her being directed to ambitious schemes and projects to be realised in the future by her adored pupil. Her devotion to the Princess May was unremitting; and Queen Mary's association with her governess never ended until the end of Madame Bricka, which came in the year of the War. It was invariably Bricka who dined or lunched with Queen Mary when King George was absent from Buckingham Palace, and together they would renew the past, and discuss the present.

In person, Madame Bricka was tall and dark, and not very prepossessing to look on. Her attractions were rather of the mind than of the person. She was an exceptionally well-read and cultured woman (qualities not always incidental to governesses of those times). Moreover, she was, I am informed, extremely cosmopolitan in her outlook, having a considerable knowledge of the world and matters remote from the ken of her pupil, all of which was tempered by a philosophical and faintly ironical attitude toward things in general.

In her outlook, too, she was extremely radical; and Madame Bricka never seems to have made any attempt to conceal her views in that markedly Tory atmosphere at White Lodge. Her views, like her temperament, frequently "clashed" with members of the Duchess of Teck's train; and in the clash, she, the Alsatian, was unusually indulged.

Madame Bricka's influence over her young pupil was not a personal influence in the ordinary sense of the term; rather she worked through her pupil's mind, guiding, directing, feeding, and replenishing that eternally enquiring and observing instrument, well calculated to have greatly exercised a less informed or intellectual woman than Madame Bricka. The Alsatian governess, however, was dauntless and more than equal to the exacting requirements of her royal pupil, who, even at the earliest age, was not easily put off with vague answers.

Madame Bricka did not conspicuously shine for her own personal tact in the negotiation of daily life. There were people who definitely did not like her—a state of affairs which left her notably cold and unmoved. Her concern seems to have been rather in the development and furnishing of her pupil's mind rather than in laying herself out to please those with whom she came into contact; and though she did not develop or exercise her own tact, she saw to it that her pupil, destined to adorn some high social position, should not be without the blessed lubricant. She taught by precept, where example failed. And she had the inherited "social sense" often found in a frontier race.

Bricka, the exacting, could not have demanded of the gods a pupil more after her own heart than Princess May—one more responsive, one more profitable, one more altogether worth while than the quiet, shy, reserved, amazingly courteous and deferential English girl. She held her tenaciously with heart, soul, and mind; and the embrace was not unwelcome. The education and guardianship of the English princess became a sort of religion to the Alsatian. Devotions were never more regularly performed.

With the eye of personal love, as well as the eye of a shrewd woman of the world, Madame Bricka took the measure of the potentialities in this material before her. She found a great and practical intelligence, on which no effort, no explanation, was wasted; she found artistic susceptibilities; she found a strangely marked and rather matured sense of the value of life and its possibilities; earnestness, reverence, character; and a tremendous resolution lying, for the most part, dormant. Above all, she found a great desire to learn in her pupil; and Bricka was reduced to ecstasy by the discovery.

Very early, it seems, she had resolved that a high destiny awaited her pupil; and that that pupil should not be found wanting.

Madame Bricka's first procedure has been described to me as "the revealing to Princess May the capacity of her own mind—she helped her, as it were, to discover her own self." On the basis of this excellent beginning, they set jointly to work, devoting the mornings to study and reading (Madame Bricka was a good linguist); the afternoons her pupil spent with the Duchess of Teck, accompanying her on her numberless charitable and philanthropic pilgrimages.

Both the governess and her pupil had a mutual zest for history. They read widely; and it was their habit to hold protracted discussions together on all they read. Madame Bricka, it seems, had very definite notions on the uses and value of reading, and was fond of quoting the instance of Salmasius and Grotius, as examples of how you may make a person either an enlightened philosopher, able to cope with life, or a learned pedant, stuffed with useless erudition.

Always she put before her pupil's mind an end for her reading. Nothing was hastily read; nor would she tolerate the habit of skipping from one subject to another, before the mind can settle on, much less grasp, a single idea. This slipshod method she deplored as an inconstancy that weakened concentration, confused ideas, and robbed its victims even of their common sense.

Together they read abundantly and with great attention, never admitting a conclusion without comprehending its reason; they read to pause, to reflect, to interrogate. The use of reading, Madame Bricka would aver, was also to aid in thinking; therefore it was equally fallacious to harden and contract the mind in long and exclusive application to a single subject.

All these maxims of Madame Bricka were gratefully and profitably received; and Queen Mary, it may be said to-day, has never lost that habit of reading first inculcated by her governess.

Madame Bricka more than succeeded Fraulein Gutmann, the previous governess; she established herself in the very heart of the family life at White Lodge; her passport everywhere was her absolute and single-hearted devotion to the future of Princess May. She became attached also to the Duke and Duchess of Teck.

Bricka saw the fruits of her devoted service to the Princess May; her intimations that she would some day fulfil a high destiny were more than realised. She saw her pupil as the Duchess of York, as Princess of Wales, the mother of six children, and later, as Queen Mary of England.

The value of the astringent, radical mind of Bricka in the Tory household at White Lodge should not be under-estimated; and in the pupil's attachment is the indication of a tendency of mind to be felt and realised when with King George she came to the throne of England.

The choicest morsel in the history of Richmond—to the mind of Madame Bricka—(and it is characteristic of the trend of her mind)—concerned the violation of the public rights of Richmond Park conceded by Charles II to the inhabitants of Richmond—constituting a right of way through the verdant enclosure.

These rights had been faithfully upheld by the Royal Rangers of Richmond Park until the advent of Sir Robert Walpole as Ranger, who, with imperious gesture, threw ladder stiles over the walls of the Park and instituted gates to shut out the public. This started the memorable battle between the residents of Richmond and the Ranger of the Park, protracted over long years, the results of which were so altogether pleasing to the radical mind of Bricka.

Instead of free, dignified access to the Park, according to the rights ceded by Charles I, the public had now to beg tickets of the Ranger before they were allowed access. Richmond bided its time in sulky silence.

In 1751 the rangership was given to Princess Amelia, the younger daughter of George II; and the Princess saw fit to aggravate the encroachments already started by Sir Robert Walpole. It was maintained, and the new royal Ranger stood firm by the maintenance, that the public interfered with the sports of the park. The restrictions were increased by the Princess, and an even more select few were admitted to the park.

This was intolerable; and the inhabitants of the surrounding parts promptly instituted two lawsuits with regard to the public right of way. The first suit they lost; but the second, instituted by a brewer in Richmond, John Lewis, was tried at the Kingston Assizes and won, thanks to the fortitude and justice of Sir Michael Foster, who tried the case, and the tenacity and persistence of the plaintiff, Lewis. The public right of way was again established, and upheld by all the majesty of the law; the footpath through the park was opened to the public, and has remained open ever since.

.   .   .   .   .   .

It is a fact recorded by the highly competent observer, Lady Mount-Stephen, and confirmed by Lady Eva Dugdale, that Princess May alone exerted influence over the difficult Alsatian. She had only to come into a room where Madame Bricka was exhibiting "temperament" or airing some perversity, instantly "to take the wind completely out of her sails."

IX

IT should be remembered that Queen Mary has known what it is to be poor; indeed, she is more than familiar with the poverty of those in high social place where much is looked for and there is much semblance to be maintained. The difficulties of making both ends meet in what was expected of them made her parents' lives often one continuous care.

To this state of things Princess May was, to say the least, sensitive—alive in every nerve to her parents' needs and distresses, and, for the most part, condemned to look on and suffer in silence, unable to relieve the tension and disquiet. She could only share their mortification; and this she did in such measure that it brought the soberness and responsibility of a woman to the girl in her teens.

There was nothing she could do except, perhaps, to pray and silently hope that one day her mother might desist from the delightful if uncomfortable habit of giving away "just twice as much as she could afford," when the ceaseless appeals were made to her charity. In some ways it is true she could and did scheme and, by virtue of her executive ability, succeed in cutting down a pound or two on some venture in her mother's private charities; but this only made the faintest stir in the sea of their troubles.

Queen Mary's acquaintance with poverty during the

most impressionable years of her life should always be remembered; for it explains much in her methods of philanthropy that cannot be explained by the knowledge alone of her "common sense that amounts almost to genius," her acute sensitiveness to the needs and sufferings of the poor of all classes, and that inborn courtesy with which she approaches any charitable work, a courtesy that comes from her profound humility and respect for any human being. She has personally known the inquietudes, the sheer waste engendered by want and insufficiency.

The time came when the apartments in Kensington Palace had to be abandoned by her mother. There was no longer money to keep them up, and the wrench that it caused her mother to give up the place of her early married life is pathetically evident in her letters and diary at this time. There was none of her accustomed buoyancy in this bow to the inevitable. June 6th, 1883, she is writing to a friend:

"I do my best to keep up my spirits and make myself pleasant; for, alas! a great trial is before me. On Saturday next we are going up from here to wind up there and break up the beautiful happy home that has sheltered us for the last sixteen years, and in which all our children were born. You can guess the wrench it will be to us."

Worse was to come, and, about the middle of September, 1883, after the renouncement of Kensington Palace, and all the emotional stress consequent on that renouncement, when the Queen was a girl of sixteen, the family was compelled to set forth on a more or less

Princess. When she left Richmond for Florence she was painfully shy, untried, a stranger to the bigger world outside of Richmond, finding it difficult to respond easily, hardly aware of the capacity of her own mind for the greater interests of Art and Beauty and not greatly encouraged thereto; extremely sensitive to the difficulties and complications, financial and otherwise, that harassed her mother, and having a sense of duty and responsibility which did much to sober her youth, and would have more suited an older woman.

From Florence she returned with the same wealth of fair hair, the fresh complexion—(still the envy of women who behold it)—older by two years, mentally and artistically the richer by ten or twenty years; she was softer, more assured, infinitely more confident.

The ostensibly unemotional English girl was now in the warmth of Florence, with its romance, its beauty, its remoteness from the mundane cares of Richmond. To its charms and its revelations she submitted utterly; and in submission came a great happiness. She was free; she was happy; all the day was hers to live and learn: it was delirious exile.

In the Church of San Lorenzo, the favourite of Cosimo "Pater Patriæ," first great man of the Medici, and chosen by him for his resting-place, she would wander—in rapt admiration of Brunelleschi's interior, with those more than finishing touches lavished upon it by the genius of Donatello. She halted before the resting-place of Cosimo, buried beneath the floor in front of the high altar in obedience to his wish and by special permission of the Roman Catholic Church. In the Michelangelo sacristy, the allegorical figures of

Day and Night that preside so majestically over the tombs of two of Cosimo's descendants subdued her to a new sense of the power of mind of their creator.

Florence was overwhelming; but after the first few weeks she recovered her equilibrium, and, having surveyed the city, proceeded deliberately to make it her own. She must be thorough, of course. Every book illuminating the history of Florence and its art that she could seize she retired with to her room at I Cedri to pore over and to prepare herself for the next day's excursion. She was usually accompanied on her wanderings, sometimes by her mother, again by her governess or an official of the place to be visited; whatever the circumstances, she must get the most out of every opportunity that came her way. (This habit she has never lost.) The guide must find her intelligent, keenly interested. And so the preparation went on.

Was it to the cloisters of the Recouets, in the Via Cavour, with its charming little court and beautiful frescoes in Grisaille by Andrea del Sarto and Fracciabigio that they were to visit next day? The time before starting was given to the study of the life of Andrea del Sarto, so romanticised in England by Browning in "The Faultless Painter."

There were stories she must learn of Andrea's apprenticeship to Piero di Cosimo, so distinguished by his oddities and the lengths to which he carried them; of the strange shapes that Andrea's master found in the clouds and the extremities to which his passionate pursuit of the grotesque led him for monstrous and fantastic landscapes, carrying out, with exuberant literalness, Leonardo's directions to "look hard at spotty walls for inspiration."

Vincigliata and the now ruined castle, the scene of a siege by Sir John Hawkwood at the head of his free-lances fighting for the Pisan Republic, she visited with her guide another day, committing to her diary the story of Hawkwood, the Essex man, son of a tanner at Hinckford in the fourteenth century, who reached France as an archer under Edward III, and, after many and lucrative raids on Papal Territory in Prov-ence, put his impatient sword at the service of the highest bidder among the warlike cities and provinces of Italy, ultimately passing altogether in the service of Florence and delivering her signally from her enemies.

In the entrance-hall of the Duomo she saw his por-trait painted by Paolo Uccello (whose great battle pic-ture is one of the glories of the National Gallery); and his burial-place in the Duomo, on the north side of the choir, beneath a sumptuous monument made by his own directions and adorned with Uccello's frescoes. How one of the daughters of this freebooter married John Shelley and enriched the ancestry of our own Shelley, who, it is interesting to note, wrote his "Ode to the West Wind," and his mordant satire "Peter Bell the Third" within a stone's-throw of the tomb of his illustrious and military ancestor, she learned as they explored the chambers of the old castle in the fading light, and with the help of a solitary candle, scrambled up the narrow winding tower to behold the glory of the deep crimson sunset from its battlements.

That inexhaustible capacity and endurance for seeing sights that is only too well known to all who have ever accompanied Queen Mary abroad, or on excursions at home, was with her as a girl. Here her dauntless physical strength stands her in good stead; she is never tired, never bored; at the end of the day incorrigibly ready to start over again. For these reasons she is a rare travelling companion, if an exhausting one; and in the many stories that are told of her sustained, unflagging interest over long periods of travel, the exhibition of her "uncanny memory" for places and persons, the working of her power of observation, and trained interest, one often hears the melancholy note sounded by someone who faints by the way.

She proceeds, oblivious to all but the goal before her; until some exhausted guide reminds her gently of human limitations; or until she wakes, as it were, from the spell of the chase, and realises that the party is flagging wearily behind. Once she realises that she has outwalked, and in various other ways excelled everyone else, it is well for the rest of the party!

The Duchess of Teck was no great walker; and no doubt her limitations were borne in on her as her unquenchable daughter would lead the way through the Pitti Palace, up the hill to the Boboli Gardens where the panorama of Florence and the surrounding Apennines is laid out. From this hill-side, Princess May had been informed, much of the stone from Florence was quarried before it was arranged in the dignified and nicely clipped gardens visible in the valley below; and in earlier centuries the hills formed an amphitheatre where the Florentine courtiers and ladies used to watch the court pageantries, and the peasants at work in the vineyards, and white oxen ploughing in the olive groves.

There were visits, too, that mother and daughter undertook jointly to the Marchese Ginori's Porcelain Manufactory where Marchesa Ginori and her brother-in-law, Marchese Torrigian, received the little party, showing them first the museum, with its wealth of specimens dating from the commencement of the manufactory in 1735, and the warehouses, in which all the variety of china is set out.   Here they watched the process of the manufacture from its beginnings, looked over the sculpture workshop where the reliefs after the della Robbia are made, ultimately making their way to the Ateliers, where the best artists painted the china.

Gasperi took the Princess May over the Academia delle Belle Arte in the Via Ricasoli, a street that runs like a ruled line from the Duomo to the valley of the Mugnone, where the sustained, exquisitely joyful and serene mood of Fra Angelico sets off the granite-like melancholy of Michelangelo's "David." How Michelangelo and the committee, which included Leonardo da Vinci, Perugino, Filippino Lippo, Botticelli, and Andrea della Robbia selected the site of "David"; how, by the determination of Michelangelo himself, the "Judith and Holofernes" was moved and "David" set up in its place, where it stood for three hundred and sixty-nine years, suffering only the loss of an arm broken in the Medici riots in 1572, were stories that Gasperi told her as they passed on to Fra Angelico and Fra Gionani, that Francis of Assisi in Art who, according to Vasari, "Never took up his brush without first making a prayer"; never "made a crucifix when the tears did not course down his cheek."

Meanwhile, her mother at I Cedri was fast making her house a magnet for all the surrounding Florentine families, who crowded to her informal Sunday "At Homes," showered on her return invitations, and, in short, completely took her to their hearts—as was not unusual to any company in which the Queen's mother moved.

The Princess also met people when she was not seeing something, attending some fresh wonder there; meditating in Dante's house on the celestial Beatrice who dominated the poet's life and soul; or losing herself in the church where Dante married Gemma Donati, one of the powerful Guelph family, for whom the poet seems to have cherished so scant a regard. . . .

Other days she gathered wild-flowers by Ouida's villa, and even saw Ouida "dressed all in drab," as the Duchess of Teck described the sight, driving past them in her melancholic way, and in her proud donkey carriage. She visited the Medici villa, fitted up by Lady Oxford, aunt to Horace Walpole; and from the spot watched the sun set over the mountains of Carrara.

And so the days in Florence passed—exile for the mother, ecstasy for the daughter garnering considerable artistic knowledge and a "ken of things" that has served her country so well in her custodianship of the royal homes.

X

TO the ordinary observer in a London drawing-room, there was no very marked difference in the girl who now "came out" among them than when they had met her at White Lodge, on visits to her mother, before the family retired to Florence. She had the same dignity and, apparently, the same composure which still settled into something very like stolidity the more shy she became. She was still unwilling to talk about nothing, which might seem a modest merit if it were not so uncommon. And she was two years older: a fact that left remarkably few traces in the soft, fresh complexion.

There was, it is true, a more searching look in the blue eyes—evidence to escape the ordinary observer in a drawing-room. She was as undemonstrative as ever; and at the approach of gush retired immediately into herself. Not that she was averse to a genuine compliment. On the contrary, she thrived and wonderfully expanded under a genuine "May, I do like your frock!" Only, there the matter had to end.

The day had long passed when her fits of shyness could be hid in a flood of tears. She had developed more confidence, more certainty, in the two years abroad. Never did she develop her mother's incomparable facility for solving the most "too, too dreadful situation." She entirely lacked that particular kind of social ease, but was armoured in habits and methods

which successfully prevented such situations from arising. For example: she made it a point never to be late,
anywhere.

The growth of her certainty and confidence had been
rather in realms intellectual and æsthetic than in social
contacts. Intelligent people found her a fascinating
companion who could talk as well as she could listen.

No doubt an intensive course of "spoiling" would, at
this period, have worked wonders with the retiring girl.

Her friends delighted in her; to many her very grav-
ity was a source of pleasure. Older people sought her
company; for, over and above her intelligence, she had
also a marked deference for age. Here, a natural disposition had been rigorously confirmed by her mother's
training. Irreverence, precociousness of any sort in
children and young people, the Duchess of Teck ab-
horred.

The "coming out" of Princess May was marked by
a curious personal experience—an experience which,
one is led to believe, does not come to many debutantes.
I give the experience in Queen Mary's own words:
"I suddenly discovered that I was not educated."

The discovery, it seems, appalled her; and it came
with disconcerting suddenness. How altogether ignorant she was! It numbed her; but not for long.

Strangely enough, as she soon discovered, no one
else much seemed to be aware of her horrible insufficiency! Except, perhaps, Bricka—the scornful, the incorrigible Bricka, who "had no patience ever with facile
empty-heads and their stupidities."

It was a revelation that came to many women at this
time; but not to the women among whom Princess May

was moving. There must have been a distressing new-
ness about the thought, coming as it did in the quiet
of White Lodge.

In the world outside, it is true, the whole of women's
position was undergoing a fundamental change, due
primarily to the bid for higher education which had
set in with the first half of the nineteenth century,
and had owed so much to Frederick Denison Maurice,
who founded Queen's College in 1848, and Charles
Kingsley, one of its professors.

In 1888, the year of the Queen's coming out, the
International Women's Suffrage Alliance was gestat-
ing; while the world was still looking askance at Mrs.
Henry Fawcett.

It must be remembered, however, that from all
direct, personal contact with these disturbing elements,
Princess May would be rigorously sheltered. If she
fell victim to the stealthy infection, it was in blissful
unknowing. She would, one may assume, have been
shocked at the suggestion.

The point is, however, that at nineteen she did suddenly discover that she was not educated; which in
essence might be called the whole discovery of women
in that period. It was, in itself, a sort of revolution.

To Bricka she turned in the anguished hour of her
discovery; and together, Bricka and her pupil decided
on a course of action. Naturally!

They would read no less than six hours every day.
They would embark with careful recklessness on the
whole sea of literature, giving perhaps more attention
to English history; for that was an especial joy to the
girl. Proceeding thus, she must at the end of the year

be just a little less ignorant than she was at the beginning. At least, that was how it seemed.

It is interesting and illuminating to realise that during the eight years from the time of her coming out up to the time of her marriage, Queen Mary faithfully kept to the self-appointed task of reading six hours every day. It is very characteristic.

Her Majesty has said: "I tried not to let anything interfere with my reading. Somehow, I managed to get the six hours out of every day!"

Quietly, and in dead earnest, Bricka and her pupil traced their way along the path of literature—ancient and modern. Afterwards, they discussed and appraised what they had read, keeping hold of what was useful and shedding the rest.

They never talked outside about the plan; but quietly, tenaciously held to it. Among the old writers they ranged, and among the new: Meredith, Carlyle, Froude, George Eliot, and the Rossettis; weeks and months they sedulously spent with the poets, philosophers, and historians of the past.

There would seem to have been little enthusiasm from within the family. The Duchess of Teck was never a great reader herself. She read in spasms; and once she became absorbed in a book there was no separating her from it. Then, she was oblivious to all things, including her ladies-in-waiting, each of whom could remember an occasion when they waited up until well past midnight for the Duchess to finish her book.

Her Royal Highness read temperamentally; very temperamentally. She was much given to interrupting the process of dressing in the morning for the purpose of reading when she might want to read; which explains in great part her habit of rising punctiliously at seven and making an appearance not before two-thirty.

No one suffered, however, from Princess May's six-hour session a day, unless it was Bricka, who found her highest pleasure in this particular form of suffering. Madame Bricka entered into the plan of helping her pupil to "educate" herself with a terrible zest and enthusiasm. And, of course, it had always been Bricka's conviction that knowledge and a habit of exercising the mind offered the only enduring insurance against boredom and those other irritants familiar to persons in high social places.

They read to weigh and consider. On the title-page of each new book upon which they embarked might have been inscribed Madame Bricka's philosophy of reading: "To spend too much time in studies is sloth; to use them too much for ornament is affectation; to make judgments only by rules is the humour of the scholar." It was not merely to know the story of dynasties, wars, and conquests that they took up in their course of historical reading; from their historical studies they traced the course of constitutional power, and read the story of social development. Long before it entered the dreams of anyone surrounding her that she might one day fill a high place in the annals of Great Britain, "a strong desire came over her" (I use the description given by the late Lady Wolverton, who knew her well) "to learn the meaning of some of the deep things of life, to know what had made mankind what it is; what had made her dear country what it was;

and what it behoved every Englishwoman to be and to do as a worthy citizen of this great country."

It was not easy always to find six hours for reading in days that were filled, as Princess May's days were filled, with functions and obligations incident to her mother's innumerable philanthropic interests, and days that were crowded with the social comings and goings of the debutante.   Much had to be abandoned in order that she might read.   Then, as now, she was full of the joy of living: she loved going out to parties; she loved dancing the cotillon; she loved sightseeing, and was devoted to the theatre; but much had to go by the board in the cause of education.   And much did go by the board.

When one remembers these things, there does seem to have been a notable significance in the fact that, of all the women in the British Empire, it was Queen Mary who in 1921 was invited by the University of Oxford to receive the highest honour in the power of the University to bestow; to be the first Queen of England to receive an honorary degree; and the first to appear in the precincts of the college in cap and gown.

Other queens had come to Oxford to *confer* honours; for the ancient University, as the Chancellor reminded his audience at the ceremony of the honouring of Queen Mary in March 1921, had been famous through the centuries for its fervent, sometimes fervid loyalty to the throne of England.

Queen Matilda, Eleanor of Aquitaine, Catherine of Aragon, Henrietta Maria—each had trod the ground that Queen Mary trod in March 1921.   Three times Catherine of Braganza had visited the college with her volatile husband who, on each occasion, was presented with a Bible whose lessons he seems to have insufficiently absorbed.

Queen Mary went to Oxford not only to confer honour, but to receive from the hands of its Chancellor the highest honour in its gift. It was a sign of the times heralding great changes, indeed, since Queen Elizabeth had been compelled to sit and suffer long Greek and Latin addresses that could only be tolerated by the dons who had delivered them; for when Queen Mary, walking from Balliol in her cap and gown, preceded by the Chancellor in his gorgeous golden robes, walked through the south doors flung wide for her reception, and took her seat in the Sheldonian Theatre to the fanfare of trumpets, it was to receive what no woman or Queen before had received, the degree of Doctor of Civil Law.

She who, as Oxford well knew, had set an example to the whole nation in her public life since she came to the throne, had also, by her life, raised the status of all women in the country.

"Not rashly, but generously wise; not stealing a march on her rivals, but giving them a lead. . . ." Oxford had opened the doors of her inmost sanctuary to women, granted them honours and facilities on equal terms with men. Oxford saw and spoke of the glorious fruits of the discovery that Queen Mary made at White Lodge as a girl of eighteen. Truly the seeds were sown in great secret!

Queen Mary's reply to the Chancellor's address was characteristic. She valued the honour, she said, not merely because it was the highest honour a university could give, not because it was unique; but because it enabled her to testify in this public way her interest in the cause of the education of women. She was confident that the women of the University would show themselves worthy of the great victory they had won.

For Queen Mary there was indeed another significance in the occasion. She had known what it was at eighteen to discover that she was not educated, in any sense of the word as she construed it even at that age; though she had been "educated" from the cradle.

She had come out socially at a time when the fundamental change in the attitude towards women's education was still taking place; when Bedford College for Women, Cheltenham, the North London Collegiate School for Girls, and many other ventures for the higher education of women were still somewhat daringly "new." She had come out before the need had been universally felt of elevating the career of nursing by means of still more thorough education; the very admission of nurses to the medical profession itself had been a triumph only of the early nineteenth century.

When Princess May was a girl of fourteen, Dr. Garret Anderson was still in the throes of her long, bitter struggle for the admission of women to the Medical Register of the United Kingdom.

.   .   .   .   .   .

The year of her coming out was memorable not only to Princess May, for the first time fully exposed to the revelations and new responsibilities of the social life, to its fatigues and its fatuities and the expanding influence

© *Byrne & Company*

AUTOGRAPHED PHOTOGRAPH OF PRINCESS MAY
IN THE YEAR OF HER DEBUT

THE TECK FAMILY

WEDDING GROUP AT MARRIAGE OF MAY OF TECK TO
GEORGE, HEIR APPARENT TO THE THRONE OF ENGLAND

of constantly meeting new people. It was a memorable year, too, in the society in which she moved. With the coming of the Jubilee celebrations there was a noticeable dismantling of the mourning appurtenances at Court. The more daring of the newspapers were quick to note and frank in reporting that Queen Victoria's Court no longer looked like a "mourning warehouse"; that the "invisible Queen at Balmoral" was becoming more of a living reality moving among them.

On many occasions Queen Victoria had appeared in public in the weeks that preceded and followed the Jubilee; she opened the People's Palace in the Mile End Road; she laid the foundation-stone at the Imperial Institute, Kensington; and travelled to Westminster Abbey in full pomp and ceremony, escorted by her royal Court, her royal bodyguard, representatives of all her Dominions, and a bevy of magnificent potentates from the East, to celebrate the fiftieth year of her reign.

Outside Buckingham Palace she reviewed twenty-eight thousand volunteers of London; on July 9th in the Jubilee year she reviewed ninety thousand soldiers at Aldershot; and the last, if not the least, of her memorable appearances in the year 1887 was made when she reviewed the fleet at Spithead.

Princess May also attended two or three of these public state functions as a member of the royal circle—not at all as a prominent member, rather as the daughter of her mother—in the background of the shifting canvas where she could observe without being too much observed; a position she would have chosen, had the choice been offered her. Not that she was impervious to pomp and ceremony; not that she was without ambition, or constitutionally averse to the shouts of the crowd. The flash and the clatter of armour, the colour of the military accoutrements, the stamping of the horses, the mighty show of the might of a great empire—these things stirred her blood and fired her imagination and swelled her heart, as they fired the humblest, the least conspicuous onlooker from the pavement.

It was only that she was not a considerable royal personage. By birth she stood many degrees from the throne; she was surrounded by cousins and relatives coming before her in precedence, and she was very wise and very deferential to such, with a completeness that positively irritated her friends. Already she was consummate in the art of effacing herself.

She sat quiet and still and regal. It was not her day. That was to come later when, soon after her marriage, she accompanied the Duke of York to Ireland and was for the first time the centrepiece of a great public show. On this occasion, Lady Eva Dugdale has told me, the seemingly unemotional young woman "wept tears of joy."

During the time of the great social beauties Princess May came out, when a debutante outside the royal circle had much to compete with; days when, says a vivacious chronicler of the times, "London worshipped beauty like the Greeks. I have seen great and conventional ladies like Lady Cadogan and others standing on iron chairs in the park to see Mrs. Langtry pass, and where Georgiana, Lady Dudley, drove, were crowds round this vision of beauty holding a large Holland

umbrella over the head of her invalid husband.
Crowds of beauties like the Moncrieffes, Grahams,
Conynghams, Mrs. Arthur Sassoon, Lady Dalhousie,
Lady Londonderry, and Lady de Grey were to be seen
in the salons of the eighties—led by Queen Alexandra,
then Princess of Wales, with her perfect oval face,
frownless brows, and the carriage, and above all the
grace both of movement and gesture which made her
the idol of the people. . . ."

The fashionable world centred about King Edward
VII and Queen Alexandra, then Prince and Princess
of Wales, and had Newmarket for its headquarters.
Rank was considered highly in those days, with the
line finely drawn between the social grades, the inner
circle being small and rigorously exclusive. The ladies
dined very late, did not smoke; and rode their horses
in Rotten Row between ten and twelve. They attended
magnificent balls in the intervals of sitting to the fashionable artists of the time—Millais, Whistler, Burne-
Jones, Poynter, and Watts; and plentifully adorned
London's two opera-houses—Covent Garden and Her
Majesty's, with Patti at the one, and Christine Nilsson
at the other, both stars in their zenith. The opera-
houses, too, were centres of fashion and beauty.

Of the painters in their meridian at this time, Princess
May became best acquainted with Sir John Millais, the
frank, manly, genial sportsman, as much devoted to
hunting and fishing as to his art and to his family.
Millais had been a baronet at the suggestion of Mr.
Gladstone a year or two before he met his youthful
admirer. It was much later that he succeeded Sir
Frederick Leighton as President of the Royal Academy.

In Princess May Sir John found a modest beginner well versed in Florentine art, very eager to acquire all that he might tell her in his bluff, broad, hearty way. At the time of their meeting he was painting his third portrait of Mr. Gladstone. Among his famous earlier sitters he could number the Marquess of Salisbury, Lord Rosebery, the Dukes of Devonshire and Argyll, Cardinal Newman, Carlyle, Sir James Paget, Sir Henry Irving, John Bright, Tennyson, and Disraeli, and could entertain the Princess with his store of anecdotes about them. In her ears also Sir John was wont to pour out tales of the woeful ills that had resulted from his series of child portraits, Cherry Ripe, Miss Muffet, and Bubbles; how his life had become one long effort to repulse the overtures of well-meaning persons who had discovered for him the most "too, too adorable children," for his models.

With her mother and occasionally with a girl friend Princess May went almost every summer to St. Moritz. Abroad, as at home, by virtue of her mother's popularity, she had exceptional opportunities for meeting interesting people. At St. Moritz she met Browning, then in a graceful old age, having survived the Browning Society founded early in the eighties by Dr. Furnival and Miss Hickey. It was during the time that Browning was foreign correspondent of the Royal Academy, after the marriage of his son in Venice and before he had moved to De Vere Gardens. Like everyone else who came in contact with the venerable poet, Princess May was much impressed by the extreme simplicity and quiet dignity with which he accepted the homage and adulation of his increasing numbers of admirers.

Browning proved himself an admirable talker; and took obvious pains to talk his best. He abounded in anecdotes, and would delight his hearers by frequent pugnacious flashes that added much keen brilliancy to his speech.

Browning seems to have been the only star in the firmament of letters at that time whom Princess May met; though Ruskin, loaded down with University degrees, and memberships of various institutions and academies, was spending his twilight at Brentwood writing the final chapters of those naïve, pathetic memories *in Præteria;* Tennyson was much alive, though eighty, and had been made a peer at the conclusion of his tour with Gladstone round the North of Scotland, to the Orkneys, and across the sea to Norway and Denmark, where the distinguished travellers had been fêted by the King and Queen of Denmark in Copenhagen.

At St. Moritz Princess May and her mother stayed at the Hotel Victoria, where were always interesting people, and where, among others, Princess May first met Miss Mary Moore and Charles Wyndham. Henry Irving and Ellen Terry she had already become acquainted with at Richmond. At St. Moritz also she met one who left a lasting impression on her mind. This was Stanley, the explorer, and finder of Livingstone, who had discovered the source of the Congo and generally accomplished more than any other explorer in Africa, with which continent his name was indissolubly linked.

The story of Stanley's romantic life, his rise from a

haberdasher's and then a butcher's shop in Liverpool; his cabin-boy days on a sailing-ship from Liverpool to New Orleans, where he was adopted by a merchant and sent to a country store in Arkansas, and his subsequent enlistment in the Confederate Army during the Civil War, was as familiar to Princess May as to the whole of England.

Most of Stanley's great accomplishments were behind him when they met; his trek in search of Livingstone in Ujiji and his navigation with Livingstone of the northern shores of Tanganyika. It was after he had accompanied Wolseley's Expedition to Ashanti and had germinated the seeds of the foundation of the Congo State.

I am indebted to Lady Wyndham (Mary Moore) for a vision of Princess May in the days of St. Moritz and the Hotel Victoria, where regularly every year she repaired with her mother for the summer months.

Sir Charles and Lady Wyndham were proud to be included in that wide circle of devoted friends which surrounded Queen Mary's mother. Her Royal Highness seems to have dominated every scene and gathering with her abounding presence and gay laughter. It was the same at St. Moritz.

Princess May was "very shy," but seems to have succumbed to the *joie de vivre* of Sir Charles Wyndham; and with him she considerably expanded.

Of after-dinner games, most popular was "Mrs. McGullicudy's Family," which seems to have provided visitors at the Hotel Victoria with endless fun and amusement. Half of the dinner guests went out of the room, half remained within, putting handkerchiefs on their heads to distinguish the McGullicudy family. Those outside the door were called in one at a time to guess a word about which they might question the McGullicudy family, who also might act the word.

"Only an idiot would think of a word like that," burst out Mary Moore one night, much provoked by Sir Charles Wyndham's repeated "I thought you had more intelligence than that!"

"Really," said Sir Charles, "it was Her Royal Highness's suggestion!"

.   .   .   .   .   .

In 1886, soon after Princess May's début, her mother took a small house in Berkeley Square belonging to Lady Ann Murray. The Duchess of Teck had been no little frightened by what Queen Mary now refers to as "the long drive home from London to Richmond," which always awaited them at the end of every party, ball, dance, or dinner that the debutante attended. It was a small house; but at least it was in London.

Gladstone and Parnell were the two dominating figures in the political world, the topic of conversation at most dinner-tables, with the question of Ireland again made a palpitating issue by Mr. Gladstone's conversion to Home Rule. There came an interval when the tragedy of Gordon at Khartoum shifted the scene of interest from Ireland to Egypt and the Mahdi.

Princess May saw a little, but not much, of Mr. Gladstone, throughout this stormy political time. Her family's sentiments were extreme Tory, and though she herself had no political prejudices, their Tory sympathies were sufficient to explain the occasional nature of her meetings with Gladstone. She did, however, dine with the Liberal Prime Minister on one occasion: an event which she recalls easily nowadays in her reflections on the period, as she recalls the fall of Mr. Gladstone's Parliament which followed the formulation of his new attitude to Home Rule; the return of the Conservatives in an overwhelming majority; and the Parnell Commission, set up to investigate the matter of the Piggott letters, which had implicated the Irish leader in the Phœnix Park murder.

Of political celebrities during the year of her coming out and after, Lord Salisbury, who followed Gladstone as the Tory Prime Minister, was better known to Princess May. The last party of her first season was at Hatfield, the home of the Salisburys since the time of Elizabeth.

This event closed her first year out, and had followed on festivities at Ashridge and a few days at Windsor. Writing of the ball at Hatfield, Princess May said: "Really, quite the nicest house I have ever stayed in. The ball was delightful, and we enjoyed ourselves thoroughly."

Lady Ann Murray's house in Berkeley Square was abandoned, and, in 1887, the Duchess of Teck took another house in Grosvenor Place for the London season. This also was a small house to fit the narrow means of the family.

.   .   .   .   .   .

To visit the homes of her mother's large circle of friends in town and country was a constant source of pleasure to Princess May; and to her mother's host of friends it was a rare joy to have Princess May with them. She was a desirable guest, ever courteous; she "put no one out," was never at a "loose end," and could always be trusted to entertain herself when the need arose. Again, she took such "quiet, thoughtful pains to please her hostess—to help in anything that arose"; and she was so capable.

With Lady Ashburton she stayed frequently. Louisa, Lady Ashburton, wife of the second Lord Ashburton, was by birth a Mackenzie of Seaforth. To her great beauty and charm was added an intelligence that enabled her to carry on many of the social traditions of her more famous predecessor. Her husband's first wife, Lady Harriet Montagu, had been the great friend of the Carlyles, and Carlyle himself continued an intimate of the house of the second Lady Ashburton.

At the Grange, Hampshire, Louisa, Lady Ashburton, held her "Court," in what Carlyle described as "the perfection of an English country palace," though the habits of the "palace" did not altogether suit the sage, with "no breakfast till ten—nothing to do." But, adds Carlyle, "the park is beautiful, the riding delightful, the solitude and silence divine. The house is built like a Grecian Temple, of two stories, of immense extent, massive in appearance and fronting every way. The interior is by Inigo Jones, with modern improvements. The rooms are full of exquisite pictures, and there is every convenience."

The historic Rufford Abbey, in Nottinghamshire, is another of Queen Mary's happy memories of the years after her coming out, before her marriage. Mr. Augustus Lumley, the second of three unmarried brothers who in turn succeeded to the historic Abbey, was her host and a great friend of her mother's. He was a man of artistic tastes, famous as a leader of cotillons, a prominent and popular figure in London during the seventies and eighties. His great kindness of heart commended him to all, including Princess May.

Rufford Abbey, originally a religious house for Cistercian monks, founded by Gilbert de Gaunt, Earl of Lincoln, in 1148, and granted by Henry VIII to the Earl of Shrewsbury and Waterford in exchange for estates in Ireland, appealed greatly to the historic sense of Princess May, with its entrances by a massive gateway erected by the eighth Earl of Scarborough, through which and beneath a fine avenue of lime, beech, and elm trees, approach is made to the ancient abbey buildings of Rufford.

From Rufford Abbey Mr. Augustus Lumley would conduct his royal guest on tours of the surrounding country and its places of historic interest; and for such excursions she had a great capacity. To Welbeck Abbey they went, the home of the Duke of Portland, founded by Thomas de Cuckney in 1154; visited its famous orangeries, pine-pits, vineries, conservatories, and Princess May abandoned herself to its vast collection of magnificent pictures. Little is left of the conventual building at Welbeck; but there are still fascinating evidences of the fifth Duke, a recluse who is responsible for the underground picture-gallery and ballroom at Welbeck, long accepted as the "largest and in every way most luxurious private room in England"; the subterranean passages, apartments, kitchens, and pantries for the supply of food are further results of the same strange hobby for underground structure.

From Welbeck they visited Thoresby, the home of Lord Manvers, a lofty building in the Elizabethan style, the third of its kind to be erected there; an earlier structure had been the birthplace of Lady Mary Montagu, Queen of the Blue-stockings.

Clumber House, the chief seat of the Duke of Newcastle, was also included in Princess May's tours from Rufford Abbey. There she made some slight acquaintance with one of the finest libraries in the kingdom, and admired as well the princely collection of paintings wherein Rubens, Hogarth, Gainsborough, and Rembrandt were each well represented.

As a girl of thirteen, Queen Mary went first to visit the Hopetouns, who were among her mother's most intimate friends. "Then it was," Her Majesty has said, "that I got to know and love Scotland." With that "uncanny memory," the Queen can vividly recall her first happy days in Scotland and Edinburgh—the visit to Holyrood, the Holyrood that now owes so much to Her Majesty's unremitting care.

It is interesting to reflect how little she knew in those days of what the future held in store for her with regard to Holyrood—that a day would come when she should be custodian also of the High Commissioner's quarters there, and, with soul outraged at the neglect into which the palace had fallen, would "tuck up her sleeves" and set about turning the place "inside out."

At Holyrood, but only at Holyrood, it can truly be said that Queen Mary actually does tuck up her sleeves!

Holyrood hardly knows its own self to-day—thanks to Queen Mary, who could hardly have suspected when she was "learning to love Scotland" at thirteen, a guest of the Hopetouns, that she would one day be called upon to turn her love to intensely practical account.

Stirling, second to no place in Scotland for historical interest, she also visited, to survey from its eminence on the Forth the main passage from the Lowlands to the Highlands—a strategic position of importance to the city as capital of Scotland from the days of Malcolm Canmore to the reign of James VI. She looked over the picturesque town from "Victoria's Look-out," on the upper court of the Castle, rising above Stirling on a precipitous crown of hills, further strengthened by two walls and fosses, which give the Castle a superb situation for military purposes as well as for the view it commands of the surrounding country in all its rugged glory.

Dunfermline, which succeeded Iona as the burial-place of the Scottish Kings, was also a part of those youthful visits to the Hopetouns in Scotland made in two successive years during the summer holidays; once to convalesce from an illness that had left her weak and, according to her mother, "growing alarmingly tall"; the second time to join in the celebration of the coming of age of the Earl of Hopetoun's son and heir, who, in after-years, acted as host to the young visitor when she was Duchess of York, accompanying her husband on the colonial tours, when they paid their State visit to Australia.

. . . . . .

It was a happy year, the year of Princess May's coming out. It closed dramatically; and with an experience of deeper import to the future Queen Mary of England than cotillons and country house visits, delightful as they were, and, to none at that time, more delightful than to her. She came sharply, unforgettably in contact with the East End of London in its stark misery and desolation; and the shock of the impact was deep and enduring.

One dwells on it, for it explains so much about Queen Mary that is otherwise inexplicable.

Wherever Queen Mary has visited the east side of our cities, wherever she has been directly or indirectly associated with reforms and philanthropies touching the welfare of those who dwell East and labour there, certain facts, certain circumstances stand out clearly in the minds of all who have been associated with her in these undertakings. One here will tell of Queen Mary's vision and intense longing to help in a practical manner; another dwells wonderingly on her intimate knowledge of industry and industrial conditions; of her disconcerting questions relating to matters behind what she is being shown at the moment; of her eagle, all-observing eye and the impossibility of putting her off what she is intent on knowing concerning the welfare of the workers, and the conditions in which they work; above all, of her entire freedom from the remotest suggestion of the Lady Bountiful.

Many a factory owner has wondered, as he escorted the royal party round, whether it was quite seemly for a Queen to know so much; certainly, this disconcerting intelligence is not, in the popular imagination, associated with high place and regal persons when they descend to walk in lower regions.

Queen Mary's knowledge of what are known as the labouring classes, the unusual method of her approach to them and all that concerns them, the genuineness of her understanding, and her sympathy with them, may be illuminated no little by the strange adventure that befell her as a debutante, in the midst of her social round and revelry, and the executive work incident to her mother's countless charitable interests which, as a girl, she always undertook—for the reason that she alone was the most competent to plan and scheme and organise.

The adventure explains in great part the shock to their beliefs, no less than to their prejudices, that Labour men and women almost always sustain when first they come in contact with Queen Mary, and experience the reach of her knowledge, no less than the acuteness of her sympathy with the poor—her "sterling good sense and clear point of view," as a Labour leader once summed her up to me, "her entire absence of sham and absolute sincerity."

It will no doubt help the royal bootmaker to understand why, in his memorable encounter with the royal lady when he was fitting her for some embroidered shoes, she was able to discourse, not without irony, on the unhappy women who made the embroidery for so many shoes in the East End of London, and the strange discrepancy between what they are paid and the maker receives, when the shoes are finished and sold. It explains, too, her preoccupation at that early age with official parliamentary literature, and why the lady, call-

being. With point and the profus
pointed out how the sweating dens
soil for small-pox and the breedir
so easily spread abroad by the garm
pence in the East End and sold i
London. Once this fact was fully
nence of disease spreading from t
the East to the innocent homes of t
tion for an enquiry into the Sweat
sufficient volume and power to for
liament, and resulted in the Sele
posed of the Lord Archbishop of C
of Derby and Onslow; the Lords
Chudleigh, Limerick, Crawford, D
Rothschild, Monkswell, and Thr
Dunraven was appointed Chairma

Two hundred and ninety-one w
the East End of London to Westi
dence of their miserable state:
cabinetmakers; sweated workers fr
nail-making industries at Cradle
shirt and mantle makers; worker
stery, cutlery, and hardware manu
labourers, represented by Ben Till

The findings of the Select Comm
impression on Princess May, who
incredulity, and her customary pur
tion, followed the evidence day by
lished in the newspapers. To rea
columns now is like reading out
Dostoievsky. The witnesses gave
a bleak economy of words and emot

ing at White Lodge, found her absorbed in a Blue Book on the State care of the mentally afflicted.

That the experience could have been a horrible adventure to a girl brought up as Princess May had been brought up, conveys a great deal.

Princess May, at nineteen, was not unacquainted with "the poor." Sir Clement Kinloch-Cooke, in his review of the attitude of the Duchess of Teck with regard to the upbringing of her children, has observed that: "In order that Princess May and her brothers might fully realise the needs of others . . . on one occasion the Duchess sent a dinner to a destitute family (in the vicinity of Richmond) and gave instructions that the children were to stop and see the poor people enjoying their meal."

Edifying, no doubt, as the experience must have been, it could not be said to have prepared Princess May for the shock of her encounter with the "Select Committee," appointed by the House of Lords in 1888 to enquire into the sweating system in the East End of London—the encounter which represents her first real encounter with the life of the poor.

The findings of the Select Committee appalled not only Princess May, the self-appointed systematic and serious student of life at White Lodge, Richmond. They thoroughly startled the public, and at least for a few weeks diverted interest from the rarefied atmosphere of the "Souls," the turgid struggles of women for political franchise and professional opportunities— the superæsthesia of the Æsthetes, the milk baths of the Beauties, the troubles in Ireland, and the convulsions

of Madame Blavatsk
following.

Over a period of e
mittee sat, examining
workers, who trekked f
chapel, and Bethnal G
Lords of their starvati
their average working
who worked with then
a story of disease an
misery as made the L
seats, and on one notab
an extremity that they
due and proper escort
wretched hovels of the

Kingsley and his frie
begun the agitation w
the Select Committee
would have gone a ha
foreseen the legislation
and his own vigorous
Alton Locke, which u
goal until nearly forty

Slumming was not t
there a few fine souls I
Barnett took up their r
Tower Hamlets for th
recreation, and knowle
only a few lonely souls
and starvation. It was
of a bright journalist,
narrative that the Sele

sionally by the passionate oratory of one or two social
workers and writers, and the Secretary of the Jewish
Board of Guardians, who was among the first to be
called before the Lords.

Princess May, unlike the majority of people who
followed the gruesome story unrolled before the Select
Committee, was not entirely dependent on the news-
paper accounts. The Earl of Dunraven, Chairman of
the Select Committee, was a near neighbour, living in
Richmond, and a great friend of the Duke and Duchess
of Teck; and from him Princess May was able to fill
in the details of the picture omitted by a considerate
press. From Lord Dunraven she sought and obtained
fuller facts and information. Lord Dunraven also enlightened her on obscure points of the evidence, and
the technical difficulties involved in the legislation to
break up the sweating system.

Princess May was now twenty-one; and she had
never before conceived of human misery and distress
on the scale and magnitude of this revealed to the
Select Committee day by day in the House of Lords.
She was appalled—horrified—helpless—and snatched
her studies abruptly from Froude, Macaulay, Ruskin,
Rossetti and the Elizabethans (her interest in the
Elizabethans had been renewed through a course of
lectures delivered at Richmond by Churton Collins,
which she had attended), to the more practical and
prosaic theses on social reform.

Like many another sensitive soul of the time, Princess
May was haunted by the haggard faces of the workers
who gave evidence in person before the Committee—
such evidence as those were able to give who were not

altogether rendered dumb and stupid by hardships daily endured: Russian immigrants, like one Hyman Kreisberg, who told the Committee that he did not move from his workstool from seven in the morning until past midnight, living exclusively on bread and coffee, to earn five, six, sometimes seven shillings a week by turning and finishing boots.

One member of the Committee had actually to take a sweated worker from his seat in the sweat-shop to bring him before the Lords to tell his story of working from six in the morning until twelve at night for six shillings and sixpence a week; and the members of the Committee themselves had been taken to rooms in tenement houses in Burdett Road where mothers and fathers and families of five and six children lived, slept, ate, and worked in one single room. Another witness, one Mary Hayes, a widow tailor, was persuaded to tell the gentlemen what food she had worked on for the last ten years, from eight in the morning until ten at night, and she had been obliged to confess that she was "ashamed" to say that she "never had meat," but lived mostly on bread and butter, with occasionally "a few shrimps."

Side by side with the immigrants from Odessa, Minsk, and the borders of Russia and Poland, caught at the various ports of landing and inveigled into the East End sweating dens where they worked from fifteen to twenty hours a day for five shillings a week, were Cockney families from the Tower Hamlets, and other unsalubrious quarters of the East End, tailoresses and mantle-makers—all come to swell the evidence with their stories of eighteen-hour days for a starvation pittance, with families of seven and eight who slept in rows in the rooms in which they worked day and night.

Lord Dunraven has told, in his autobiography, how arduous and how difficult was this first attempt, represented by the setting up of the Select Committee, to acquaint the world with the sweating system of the East End of London; and how the Committee was hampered by its inability to indemnify the witnesses against possible losses, the reluctance of many witnesses to give evidence that might then, or in the future, prejudice their prospects; and of the inability of so many of the witnesses even to talk English.

He has told of poor, proud chain-makers, who borrowed clothes from their friends in order to put in a respectable appearance at the House of Lords to tell their terrible stories; of the hard-faced members on that Committee thoroughly imbued with the "Manchester School" theory of cheap labour, and their constitutional repugnance to the very idea of a living wage, and of their wont to propound questions involving profound problems of political economy to these poor, starved, ignorant men and women who knew nothing of such niceties, and understood as much as if they had heard a discourse in ancient Greek.

How hard it was to get these workers even to say how they were housed, fed, and paid, Lord Dunraven has also told; how "delightful" they were, and so "greatly to be respected"; how "impressed" he was by the way they gave their evidence, and their manifest desire to minimise the effect of all the horror that they were telling.

The Committee, as is known, would not accept Lord

Dunraven's report—it was rejected even as a draft for consideration, and, in consequence, Lord Dunraven resigned. The actual legislation which came out of the findings of the Committee was very slight, and related mostly to improvements in sanitation. But although the direct results were disappointing, public opinion had been awakened, and the affair as a whole was a gesture in the direction of industrial reform which, later, with the organisation of powerful Trades Unions, proved so effective.

Henceforth, blue books and like literature became a great part of the Princess May's daily diet, and under the composed exterior something in the nature of a revolution was taking place. Lord Dunraven's experience of officialdom and red tape was by her, too, assimilated, quietly but very thoroughly digested, as will be seen later.

XI

IN her twenty-fifth year Princess May was engaged
to the Duke of Clarence, heir presumptive to the
throne of Great Britain. Two months after the announcement of the betrothal, five weeks before the
date fixed for the marriage, the Duke of Clarence died
at Sandringham during an epidemic of influenza.

To the country at large the shock was severe and distressing; the whole world lamented the fact of this
young life cut off in the early twenties. Mr. Gladstone
wrote to Sir William Harcourt at the time: "The
nation's grief resembles that on the death of the
Princess Charlotte. . . ."

Queen Victoria was stunned; and among the numerous letters that she wrote from Balmoral on the crest
of her grief, was one to the poet Tennyson:

"Was there ever a more terrible catastrophe? A
wedding with bright hopes turned into a funeral." In
an address to the people she referred to her grandson's
death as "one more sad and tragical than any but one
that has befallen me. . . ."

The Duke of Clarence was buried in St. George's
Chapel, Windsor; and of that melancholy event in
the minds of those now living remains one fixed and
enduring memory; the memory of Princess May,
dressed in the deepest mourning crape, her colour fled,
her eyes fixed in remotest space, her face white and

tense, taking her place dry-eyed among the weeping mourners, without even the solace of tears.

It was her first intimate shock, and one that she had to sustain before the eyes of the world; but it was not her first pain. Always she had been sensitive; and this had brought her suffering; often she had been loaded with responsibilities that, possibly, belonged to others, and certainly were not meet companions for her years.

Family troubles and vicissitudes she had to an unusual degree made her own. The necessity for her, at least, to be practical had been early and persistently brought home to her; and the impractical had put cares upon her with characteristic ruthlessness. She could always be trusted to bear things well, and never to make a scene—an accomplishment that she had achieved, and that was always conveniently mistaken for a natural gift which she had inherited in the cradle. Our "sweet Mayflower," as her mother continually referred to her in her letters to friends, was also something of a rock of Gibraltar.

Immediately after the funeral of the Duke of Clarence Princess May retired with her mother to the seclusion of White Lodge; but seclusion there was none from the hysterical demonstrations of unknown sympathisers who intruded upon her grief on every public occasion, and indefatigably ventilated it in the columns of the press, moved, it would seem, by a fixed determination to make of her a never-failing fountain for the fiction-writers of the day.

Unfortunately for these romantic-ridden minds, Princess May was of all things a sincere, genuine, and

upright soul, possessing a healthy mind.   There was
no sackcloth and ashes; only a very quiet demeanour,
and a rather pained look in her eyes that much discomposed people who peered curiously into them.

And she was twenty-five, full of the joy of life!

From her close retirement at Richmond she went
abroad with her mother and Lady Wolverton to the
South of France.   What she felt and what she thought
in the first sharp experience that life had brought her,
and in the long quiet days that followed, at Richmond
and in France, did not altogether pass away with her
grief.   When her own children came, and grew up,
she was deeply understanding.

On May 3rd, 1893, the engagement was announced
of Princess May and Prince George, now her presumptive to the throne.   On the morning of the publication of the announcement *The Morning Post*
remarks in its leading article:

"The marriage of one who is the ultimate heir to
the throne is not an event which can be regarded as
purely of a private character.   At the same time, the
day has long since passed when the spectacle of a
future monarch seeking in his spouse merely some
princess who might furnish a great figure-head of state
would be regarded with satisfaction by loyal Englishmen.   On this account alone, then, the felicitations
offered to the Duke of York will be both spontaneous
and sincere.   He is fortunately able to please himself
and to delight the nation at the same time by the choice
of a Princess whose name has a sympathetic charm for
all, and whose future will be followed by all with constant interest.   She is essentially a daughter of Eng-

land; for it must not be forgotten that as a great grand-daughter of George III she herself stands, howbeit remotely, in the line of succession to the throne. More, not only by birth, but by education and by domicile, she belongs to England. She possesses every qualification for the high place that awaits her. . . ."

Two facts had taken firm hold of the imagination of the nation, emphasised in every public and private congratulation that flowed into White Lodge from all over the world: One, that Princess May was "essentially a daughter of England," the second that the "Sailor Prince" had "made his own choice."

It is an accepted fact that, in the opinion of Queen Victoria and King Edward, Princess May was the fittest of women to be one day Queen of England. King Edward was a shrewd, if reticent, judge; he discerned the calibre and quality of Princess May, and was not always silent about it.

The engagement was made on May 3rd, when the Duke of York visited White Lodge and remained to dinner with the Duke and Duchess of Teck. He afterwards went to East Sheen House, the residence of the Duke of Fife, where he stayed the night. On Wednesday morning he immediately set out for Balmoral, where Queen Victoria was in residence; and from Balmoral, on Wednesday evening, the Queen signified from the Highlands that: "Her Majesty received this evening the news of the betrothal of her grandson to Princess Victoria Mary of Teck, to which union the Queen has gladly given her consent."

Meanwhile the Grand Duchess Augusta had left

Strelitz for England to be with her "Mayflower," at Richmond.

Cordial messages from all the sovereigns of Europe reached White Lodge the day after the announcement had been made in England. From America, too, came congratulations, couched in warmest terms, and with the practical reminder that this was the first time since the reign of King James II that the heir presumptive to the British throne had been betrothed to an English princess—an historical calculation which, apparently, Englishmen had not recovered sufficiently to make.

There were, however, other elements in the reception —discreetly summed up by *The Times* in its leader on the morning of the announcement of the engagement:

"We have the satisfaction of making the announcement for which the public will not be wholly unprepared," it said. "The understanding so long reported to exist between the Duke of York and Princess May has now taken the form of a definite betrothal, which has received the ready sanction of Her Majesty, the Queen. We are certain that this intelligence will be received with sincere gratification. In the peculiar circumstances attending such a union there must perforce be present in every mind a certain conflict of emotions. But the predominant feeling now that a sufficient interval has elapsed since the melancholy death of the Duke of Clarence will be that this betrothal accords with the fitness of things, and, so far from offending any legitimate sentiment, is the most appropriate and delicate medicament for a wound, in its nature, never wholly ineffaceable. There is even ground for hoping that a union rooted in painful

memories may prove happy beyond the common lot.
. . . The persons of both parties are such as to attract
sympathy. On the one hand, the Duke of York enjoys
not only the popularity attaching to the Navy, but also
a personal good-will, founded on his own frank and
manly bearing on the few occasions when he has come
before the public. The Princess May is endeared to the
public by her personal charm and her amiable disposition, by the memory of her bereavement, and still more
by the devotion she displayed during that trying juncture. . . ."

With that unerring instinct which can dispense with
precise knowledge, the people of England more than
trusted and believed in their "essentially English
Princess." Prince George was a sailor, "frank, manly,
and unaffected"; and what finer passport did any Englishman ever have to the hearts of the English? They
wanted Princess May for the future Queen; Prince
George was heir presumptive to the throne. Queen
Victoria, shrewd, acutely observant, intensely jealous
for the throne of England and the might of the Empire, discreetly made no secret of her own desire for
Princess May as a granddaughter. And so there came
to pass what a noble English gentleman and a great
statesman has described: one of the "most fortunately
happy events that ever befell the English nation"—
the marriage of Prince George and Princess May of
Teck.

At Kew and Richmond "We loved her for her own
sake, and for the sake of the dear, warm-hearted
mother, the idol of everyone, high and low, whose
kindness and sympathy knew no bounds"; where "we

watched her grow up to womanhood always with the silent hope that some day she may be our Queen, and when fate seemed once again to dash that cup from our lips, we waited, not believing that a people's desire was to be frustrated," the "bright summer day" came at last. All over Richmond the parish bells rang; the flag was run up on the ancient tower; cannons were fired and everywhere flags displayed.

After all, she belonged to them; she had grown up in their midst. The occasion was more than worthy of an Address which the good people of Richmond were not backward in putting together, and presenting to her at Cambridge Cottage, the home for so long of her grandmother, the Duchess of Cambridge. Princess May was moved by the genuineness and warmth of their greeting; and in reply to the Address made her maiden speech:

"It is with sincere pleasure that I have listened to the words which have just been read," she said, "and I wish to say that I thank you most truly and very deeply for the congratulations that you have offered me. The reference that you have made to my grandmother and mother, as also to other members of my family, and to the early days of my life, in great measure passed among you, has touched me much. And I can assure you that I shall always remember this occasion and the kindness shown to me by my old friends at Kew, to whom I beg you to convey my warm thanks for their good wishes."

The Queen is not a speech-maker. No woman in her great position, called upon almost every day to adorn some public or philanthropic occasion, made fewer speeches—or more effective ones. Her words are few, absolutely sincere, and not delivered with facility. I have never spoken to a Labour man or woman who ever came in contact with the Queen personally, or as part of an audience, who did not first and last convey to me the deep impression that her remarks and speeches had made upon them.

When they had expected the usual pleasantries that are passed down from one bazaar opener to another, they were intelligently asked about things that acutely mattered to the bazaar—the baby home, or institution in question. For a formal event, they had formally prepared; only, they had not made provision to receive someone intensely and personally interested in the business at hand; and such essential respect for their work and their interests has, on more than one occasion, reduced a slumberingly belligerent Labour woman to the flutterings of a suburban hostess, suddenly surprised by royalty.

From her mother, the Duchess of Teck, Princess May had early formed the habit of looking to British manufacture for the materials and making of her clothes. So the trousseau was collected on the principle that "all the silk should come from England, all the flannel from Wales, all the tweeds from Scotland, and every yard of lace and poplin from Ireland." The Queen has never once departed from this principle laid down before the collecting of her trousseau; and in addition to her practice of patronising all British manufactures for her personal needs, has a mighty and unshakable faith in the superiority of those goods. In these matters she is guilty almost to excess of that patriotism which says: "My country, good or bad!"

It remains to be said that Princess May was not unaware of comments made in certain quarters, as she had not been unaware of the importunate public matchmakers who, at her emotional expense, would not allow the funeral baked meats to cool before they hurried on the wedding feast.

That she should suffer from this was inevitable to one so acutely sensitive. She had the sense, the wisdom, the knowledge of the world enough to know that it had created a circumstance that would be hard to outlive. This she bore with her quiet, superb largeness of mind and dignity, for explain she could not if she would: her married life itself must tell of her romance: in that should be both her reason and her justification.

And, as we know, no married life has ever been spent that more abundantly fulfilled English marital ideals than the married life of the King and Queen; to say that the breath of scandal has never once touched it is almost to be guilty of a platitude.

XII

A S Balmoral was so greatly bound up with the life
of Queen Victoria, so York Cottage, Sandringham, is associated with Queen Mary over a period of
her life when much was wrought; where new and intimate experiences, which may contract the soul as they
may expand it, brought their discipline and revelations;
where she learned much, not easily: joyed, sorrowed,
triumphed and failed, and became the gravely thoughtful woman that she is, with her inexpressible smile.

Queen Mary has not the peculiarly tenacious affection
for York Cottage that Queen Victoria had for Balmoral; yet it was her first married home, the personal
property of her husband, a place to which he was and
is still unalterably devoted: which fact alone would always give it first place in her affections, though all the
wealth of the Cottage would look foolishly wanting
in a corner of Windsor Castle, and Balmoral, in size,
could twice contain it.

By the small lake that you may overlook from the
Cottage which, in these later years, has taken on some
of the pretensions of an island, she ate her first dinner
alone with her husband on a long, warm July evening,
to the music of evening breezes stirring the leaves.
Nature had prepared the banqueting-hall, lit up with
soft fairy lights, like stars blinking far off and fugitive
in the skies.

In the small white bedroom, above the lake—everything in the Cottage is so strikingly small compared with the bewildering if regal amplitude of Windsor Castle or Buckingham Palace—five of her six children were born; while in the Cottage nursery, more conspicuously perhaps in the schoolroom, are still the signs of the overflow and abundance of childish spirits; for the small boys who sprawled and played there, and later made the motions of early learning under the village schoolmaster, wrought more than demure cards with silk letterings in pink and green, reminding "Dear Mamma" and "Dear Lala" to "Feed my Lambs" and "Look Unto Jesus." (From "Mary" to "Dear Mamma," I must say, came an extraordinary number of the most extravagant little windmills that even Don Quixote might have tilted at.)

There, too, not far from the schoolroom and nursery, is the modest dressing-room where "little Georgie"— always so acutely appreciative of feminine charm— would sidle round the door to watch "Mamma" put on her "best frock" for a sumptuous occasion, and over the whole effect lisp his ecstatic "Oh, mamma, you look stho beautiful!"

How many stories there are, "upstairs," of "little Georgie" in his impish maturity—the family custodian of the comic spirit! There was the time when he dashed up to "Mamma" with the book of *How to Write a Letter*, given to him in the village by a boy who had that week received an ungrammatical if over-epistle in "Georgie's" best style.

He was then ten, and a tremendous sportsman, with a marked dislike for the fatigue of grammar.

Said "Mamma" significantly: "I hope you will profit by it, Georgie."

"Yeth, mamma; but it doesn't sthay everything one wants to know. It doesn't sthay how to write a love-letter."

"What can you want with a love-letter?"

"You never can sthay, mamma—never!"

York Cottage, situated in the grounds of Sandring-ham, was built by King Edward to house his staff and to receive such overflow of guests as could not be accommodated at The House. It was known for a long time as Bachelor's Cottage—a name much in keeping still with its secluded aspect, the economical lines of its architecture, and the small compactness of its interior. Though it has been twice enlarged it still remains essentially a cottage, "so very nice, but so small for my needs," as the Queen wrote to a friend. It has no garden, but stands in an exquisite spot of Sandring-ham grounds with a wealth of trees and flowering shrubs, looking out on an expanse of Norfolk country sighting the hills of Wolferton that border on the Wash. It is some three or four miles from King's Lynn; and a chain of hills run from north to south between the villages of Wolferton and Sandringham above the marshy margin of the sea, glowing with amber moss and purple heather, commanding on one side the rich marsh meadows, dotted with cattle, and on the other a stretch of wild heather broken only by the plantations of Sandringham.

It commands views of a country, rich in beeches, oaks, and silver birch; rich, too, in a profusion of wild birds, though the noble bustard that once flew across the salt marshes of Wolferton, over the heath and peaty fen, has long become extinct. It is superbly endowed with wild-flowers—soft grey tufts of crested hair-grass, wall-speedwell, with its turquoise eyes, clinging leaves of hairy rock-cress, the yellow archangel and blue-bells of Wolferton wood; velvet foxglove, lilies-of-the-valley, and the horned poppy looking out to sea. The buckbean covers the marsh with a fringed and piled web of pink and white; while masses of gorse and broom flower riotously by the roadside of the heath.

Beda relates how Felix, the Burgundian missionary, was sent by Honorius "to preach the word of life and deliver this province from its long iniquity and in-felicity"; and where Felix landed at Babingley stands the first Christian church he built. Beda also tells of the tremendous success that attended the Apostle of the East Angles in his efforts to supplant the worship of the statues of Woden, the orthodox religion of the inhabitants of Sandringham and its surrounding places when he arrived.

The Manor of Sandringham, though not perhaps rooted so far back in antiquity as other parts of Norfolk, can claim distinguished association with the scholarly Earl Rivers, who brought or instigated the arrival of Caxton with his printing press to England; and Eliza-beth Rivers, whose father, Lord Scales, held the manor before her.

It came into the possession of the royal family in the time of King Edward, who bought it from Lady Harriet Cowper as a shooting-box.

For eight years, as Duchess of York and Cornwall, Queen Mary lived at York Cottage the life of an

English country squire's wife, one by no means endowed with a superfluity of wealth, and the smallness of her home was often irksome to the mother of six growing children.   During the years that followed as Princess of Wales her life was still bound up with the Cottage, in spite of the fact that, with their new title, King Edward had presented Frogmore House to his son and daughter-in-law.   It was their "country home"; and the King's attachment to it is no secret, nor his contentment in the life of a country gentleman, for which Sandringham offers endless opportunities.   At Sandringham there always awaits them a degree of freedom. There they may and often do walk unattended either by their ladies- or gentlemen-in-waiting.   Last but not least of all the links that bind them to Sandringham is the fact that it was the permanent home of Queen Alexandra.

On the threshold of York Cottage one seems to leave Their Imperial Majesties King George and Queen Mary of Great Britain, Emperor and Empress of India, to enter the domain of a great English gentleman and his wife, who have come to greatness only because greatness lay in the plain path of duty.   The Cottage is so greatly simple; it is like a small and precious symbol of that entire simplicity of the royal family which impresses all who have been admitted to some glimpse of the "family life."

So that, when all the pomp and show of a certain glittering official ceremony is entirely lost in the mind of Mr. Ramsay Macdonald and his daughter, there remains, however, ineffaceably the vision of Queen Mary suddenly shedding her "manner" as she catches sight of the crowds from the window, and in suppressed, excited whisper calling: "George, George! come quick to the window and see the people!"

York Cottage is redolent of the full, simple, happy, domestic life of King George and Queen Mary—of the partnership so well proportioned, so capable of the humblest duties as, in the days to come, it expanded to the highest they were called upon to perform; a life so contented in repose, and one so potent in action.

There is the tiny hall, a small dining-room where, as soon as the children learned to hold a knife and fork, they sat down to lunch with their parents. Before these table accomplishments were achieved they would entertain "Mamma" and "Papa" at the "grown-up" breakfast in an interlude between their own earlier breakfast and their lessons with the village schoolmaster.

"Papa's" own room remains on the ground-floor off the hall—half study, half sitting room, where, when the fatigues and duties of the morning were over, lunch past, tea taken, and the children heading for bed, he sat with his wife, who usually knitted, not being inclined to or conspicuously good at sewing, to talk over the things of the day.

The same workman-like arm-chairs remain in the study, just one or two, and the relics of the chase are there on the wall; for the lord of this Cottage had always an antipathy to change; to having his "stuff" moved or disturbed—even a carpet changed. Here is a piece of furniture, there a picture on the wall treasured from days when, as Prince George, he stayed with his tutors and brother, the Duke of Clarence, at his father's overflow Cottage.

Upstairs, sacred from profane eyes, among the precious "stuff" which belongs to the lady of the Cottage, is a little china ornament, bought probably at a fair, which "cousin Georgie" bought her when she lived at White Lodge and he at Marlborough House. It presents a small boy and a small girl in the attitude of kissing—all in pure Victorian style—such an eloquent little emblem of devotion, all somehow part and parcel of this "incredibly devoted" married life, which began at York Cottage with their long and arduous apprenticeship for the throne of England—(it lasted nearly fifteen years)—all in such severely homespun surroundings, in such chaste simplicity.

And here began the married life of King George and Queen Mary. Shrewd critics, malevolent minds, spiteful tongues, together with the noblest of Englishmen and women who have been privileged to know of it, are absolutely at one in witnessing to its love and devotion. It contains nothing else on which "one can found a sensational story."

Here began that "extraordinary delight in each other," which, if it were possible, has strengthened with the years; that marked preference for each other's company which explains why, in the early days, King George always bounded up the stairs, and before "he reached the top you could hear him:

" 'May, where are you?' "

"Always came the same reply: 'I am here.' "

To-day at Buckingham Palace you may hear: "Fourteen days pass, and the King and Queen breakfast, lunch, and dine alone. On the fifteenth day they may together go out to dinner, or there is a guest to lunch or dinner at the Palace."

As their children grow up and marry, they "seem to cling the closer."

"I swear there is not in the whole realm a married home more pure and unblemished than the home of my people," said an equerry once in a country house in Scotland.

And someone replied:

"Is there anything not possible with such a wife as Queen Mary?"

Surely strength and great goodness alone could preserve the simplicity of this home-life in the Court of the mightiest Empire of the civilised world! It began at York Cottage, this married life; and the Cottage is its symbol.

No woman more completely immersed herself in the needs and the welfare of the man she had married than did Queen Mary, nor with a greater dignity. There was no compromise in this immolation, no shifting of responsibilities with the shifting of power. First and always, she was his wife; by his side in anxiety and despondency, consoling him, greatly ambitious for him; with mind, heart, and soul ready for his service at any moment. She shirked nothing. Always she was at his side, with that fine regal bearing which makes showiness fade out of the picture. As in public, so in private, she was proud to be always in the shadow of the man she had chosen to serve.

It was the simple, literal truth that King George spoke in his first public speech after his accession to

QUEEN VICTORIA AND THE YOUNG WEDDED PAIR

FOUR GENERATIONS—VICTORIA, ALEXANDRA, MARY
AND THE PRESENT PRINCE OF WALES

the throne: "And I am encouraged by the knowledge
that I have in my dear wife a constant helpmate in
every endeavour for our people's good. . . ."

And again, more privately, when he spoke in the
Servants' Hall of Buckingham Palace thanking the
servants for their gift on the anniversary of Their
Majesties' Silver Wedding, and reminding them of his
"beloved wife," all that he and they owed to her. Only
one or two of that company can remember the words
of that impromptu speech, for it is now only an enduring memory for them of the King's simple sincerity—and the tears it brought to Queen Mary's eyes.

.   .   .   .   .   .

The honeymoon over at York Cottage, they settled
down to the profuse official duties which came to them
as the future King and Queen of England, and the
new responsibilities. The Duke of York and Cornwall
and his wife had uncommonly little leisure. Every
year brought the ardours of a "season" in London to
be sustained. In London they lived in official quarters
forming part of St. James's Palace, and named York
House with their residence there. Later, when they
were Prince and Princess of Wales, the London home
was changed to Marlborough House. Their presence
was commanded at every state function and court
gathering; the official functions they were called upon
to perform, necessitating their presence in some part
of the British Isles far from Sandringham, are too
numerous to be recalled.

Soon after Christmas they began their journeyings

from Sandringham with the Memorial Service held at the Mausoleum, Frogmore, originally in December by Queen Victoria in memory of the Prince Consort, and afterwards in January by King Edward in memory of the Queen, his mother, who was buried at the side of her husband.

Usually the children accompanied them to Windsor, where the sombre ceremony was of a family character.

From Windsor the course was set to London for the opening of Parliament. With Easter again came a visit to Windsor and back to London until Whitsuntide. Then came a visit to Aldershot, to return again for the season in London which released them in August for Goodwood, Cowes, and, after the fatigues of a long journey to Scotland, they came back to York Cottage for Christmas.

Sandwiched between all these goings and comings were endless ceremonies, public duties, and functions incident to their rank in the royal circle; while the first year of their married life included also a visit to Edinburgh to receive the wedding gift subscribed by the city, and to open the new wing of a hospital; to Stockton-on-Tees, and other English towns and cities.

The gradual, imperceptible development of Queen Mary's character, her more and more vividly clear conception of what her country no less than her King required of her as Queen, which came in the quiet retreat of York Cottage, should be noted because it seems so much more important than the "functions and things" which devolved on her at this time and throughout her long preparation for the throne.

Queen Mary was not always the woman of great

active resolution and purpose that she is to-day; nor the one who, with such supreme tact and cleverness, guides her home, her Court, and the women of the Empire; nor was her life always one protracted sacrifice to duty; nor was she always the immensely patient, understanding, kind, humane woman who compels devotion from men and women, high and low.

All these things she learned in a hard school, in the face of seemingly insuperable difficulties, which came from within and from without. Such power as Queen Mary has to-day has not come to her without discipline; from this also come her wisdom and understanding. This is true; the love and loyalty that Queen Mary inspires in those who know her best compels a reverence from whoever may have reason to know of it, or to see it working.

Consider, only, the transition she had to make from comparative freedom to the restraints of her new position. Before, she had been free, freely moving in her mother's all-embracing, cosmopolitan circle of friends. She could not now walk out without a lady-in-waiting. And she was twenty-seven. Nor was this the least incursion on her freedom; there were a hundred and one things that could not now be "done."

She was not greatly inclined to the social life; and now she was thrust into the very heart of these rarefied regions. A social order existed, and, but for meeting people who "knew things" and "did things," it bore but little relation to her tastes and natural habits of mind. . . .

Strange that a Great War should come when this great mind was at Buckingham Palace! When Europe was disintegrating, and every throne tottering, that this woman also should be in partnership, at the helm of the Empire, to preserve the throne of England!

It is at Sandringham that one is admitted most liberally to the private life of Queen Mary, not only inside the Cottage but outside on the estates, where Queen Mary is simply the "Squire's wife"—a position which must be extremely refreshing to her and in which she seems much to expand.

Her rare humour seems to find rein here; so, too, her great power of mimicry, which now and then she exerts for the delight of some select audience (usually for the special benefit of the object of her mimicry), and not infrequently to "work off" the pomposity of some bore or to lend the redeeming touch to some fatuous official who may be agitating the villagers.

Her rendering of a village friend, "disguised as a Girl Guide," who took part in a "walk past" of the Girl Guides before Princess Mary, Viscountess Lascelles, at which Queen Mary was a spectator, will live long in the memory of the "disguised" Girl Guide.

To "walk with the guns" when the Queen, too, accompanies the guns, is a treat eagerly sought after at Sandringham; for Queen Mary has a droll wit, which comes quietly, unexpectedly, and with a mischievous sheen in the blue eyes: the sort of humour it is with which the shy are often recompensed. She is no sportswoman herself, and maintains a marked restraint about her feelings in the matter. The joy of "walking with the guns" is, for her, in the walk itself.

It is less difficult too, at Sandringham, to track the working of her simple humanity—removed as it is from the profession of religion. It is a humanity as un-egotistical as is her generosity—and as full as it is spontaneous. The Lady Bountiful attitude is utterly alien to her very constitution. Here is a very compassionate heart, moved easily by distress or suffering in any form: with it also moves her mind.

There is a servant girl in distress—one of her own household, as a matter of fact.

"Poor, poor girl!"

There is no prying—no cross-examination; just pity it evokes, and a tremendous desire to help.

All that matters to the royal mistress is the girl's extremity. She must have decent privacy; she must have assurance; as far as possible, peace of mind.

The hand of the mistress is never once seen; yet for the girl it achieves a clean, peaceful safety. So much for the present.

It will not be easy for the girl to re-enter service; to attempt to return means only further exposure. It then transpires that the girl has always inclined to nursing.

Why should she not be a nurse—a District Nurse!

There, surely, will be scope for the compassion for others that her own experience must have brought her. And she will surely be happy now, doing what she has always wanted to do?

So reasons the mistress. More; by her own private effort she makes it possible for the girl to train as a nurse, and somewhere in the British Empire is an excellent District Nurse who has reason to be grateful to Queen Mary.

So unostentatious is the "Squire's wife." "Poor Mrs.

————," she hears from the housekeeper, is dying of a particularly dread disease. "It must be lonely for her, lying there all day," and the villagers, naturally enough, "don't care to catch it." She has no visitors.

And the conversation turns again to dusting. Beyond a muffled "too terrible," there is no further comment from the mistress. Returning from some business in Sandringham that morning, Queen Mary stopped at the cottage, went straight up to the bedroom of the woman, her arms loaded with flowers she had herself picked.

It was a long time before the visitor emerged—unseen, as she had made her entrance.

That consummate tact of Queen Mary which is felt so strongly in her Court, bred as it is partly of her own acute sensitiveness and boundless consideration for other people's feelings, she brings to bear on the least detail of the village. She will take endless trouble to avoid hurting the feelings of the pettiest people, even of hurting their prejudices, in situations where, it would seem, neither feelings nor prejudices have the least right to be indulged. It should be said, of course, that she is extraordinarily successful in handling these situations; in getting things done without going over the heads of those whose business it is to see that they are done, and without stirring the least ripple on the rural calm.

So much of MIND is brought to Queen Mary's benevolence: there is always discernible a sort of masculine economy of labour and emotion. And she is so courteous. In countless small, unostentatious ways you find evidence of this courtesy; only you must seek them out. It is a courtesy founded, one feels, on an innate respect for persons: a natural courtesy, and capable of infinite pains.

There is to be a "tea-fight" in the parish room; and the Queen is coming. She is to sit at table with four or five village women perhaps from Sandringham, most likely from other far-off villages in this part of Norfolk.

A request is sent from York Cottage for the names of the women with whom she will sit at table—communicated to the organiser—the estate agent's wife, or the village schoolmaster's wife. There is an added request that the Queen may know something beforehand of the things that matter to these women—their personal affairs, a new baby, a sick husband, some piece of good or ill luck that has lately befallen them—something that it may please them to talk about familiarly so that the conversation may flow with interest, so that there may be no awkward gaps in the conversation.

It is a protective too, one might hazard, against that bane to the soul of the "Squire's wife": small talk; inconsequential chatter.

This same unfailing, inborn respect she pays to any place, institution, industry, hospital, or society to which she lends her presence. To those about her, concerned with these things, the immense, the endless trouble and study that the Queen will apply beforehand to the business of knowing about things is a source of constant wonder. She proceeds invariably on the principle that, if a thing is worth her trouble, then it is also worth a personal identification; if it is worth bearing the name of the cherished "head of the womanhood of England," then surely it is worth her time and study;

surely, here, she has a responsibility toward the country and particularly towards the people who may follow her example in the trust and belief that she will not lightly set her seal to that which is not altogether worth while.

And to her courtesy is linked a common sense which, as the great statesman remarked, "amounts to genius." You wish to form a society that will gather together the village women from all the surrounding country, at set times during the year, to create a bond between them, to give them opportunities for meetings, for common interests, for enlightenment on things of moment in the management of their own homes and in the life of the nation?

An excellent idea! is the Queen's immediate response. It has her whole-hearted support. But from the royal patron comes the one warning note: be careful that you are not thrusting upon them something which they do not want. It is possible to gather the funds; it is possible to get organisers; it is possible to get a suitable meeting-place, with time and trouble; but what we cannot give them is initiative, if initiative they lack; and without this all we do would be in vain, with all our best intentions. They must learn to do the things for themselves when the start is given from the outside. The enthusiasm must come from within.

It is the repose and simplicity of Queen Mary's life that so strongly impresses one at York Cottage; yet is it the same essentially simple woman one finds at Buckingham Palace and Windsor Castle, only more obscured perhaps in forms and ceremonies—not of her making.

Because she is so intensely human and greatly simple, the simple most easily reach her.

During the King's indisposition, not long ago, there came a letter to Buckingham Palace, addressed to "Mrs. Queen"—a not uncommon form of address. Since Queen Mary opens all her own letters, this letter also was taken down in the morning. It was a letter of condolence, saying how very sorry the writer was "that your husband has got bronchitis"; it contained both sympathy and understanding, and ended with a forceful recommendation to "rub your husband's chest with camphorated oil, when the bronchial signs appear," a thing "I always do; a remedy I have never found to fail."

"So good of her to think of me, and realise my anxiety," murmured the Queen, much moved, and tremendously grateful.

The aim was unerring: from one wife to another.

At York Cottage it is not so easy to forget the woman and wife behind the Queen. It is the "Squire's wife" who dances the quadrille and Lancers or a two-step with the village schoolmaster or gardener in the ballroom at Sandringham—who picked up chestnuts with the rest of the villagers during the War, for making oil in a factory at Lynn—to whom the villagers complain not less often than they confide—who can step in at any cottage or neighbour's house on the estate and know, first hand, about things.

It is the mother also that one learns to know in Sandringham, no less than the wife—it radiates everywhere, this "quality of motherliness," as Keir Hardie once said, summing up his delight in the company of Queen Mary.

XIII

IN the spring of 1901, eight years after her marriage,
Queen Mary, then Duchess of York, accompanied
her husband on a tour of Great Britain across the seas
in the *Ophir*. It was seven months and a half before
she again saw her four children—"David," "Mary,"
"Bertie," and "Harry" in the *Victoria and Albert*,
when it moored alongside the *Ophir*, the imperial tour
ended and Their Royal Highnesses again home at
Portsmouth.

One who was on the *Ophir* has drawn for me a picture of the children, with their eager faces uplifted to
the great vessel, frantically waving at "Papa" and
"Mamm," from whom they were separated by a glittering assembly of important officials, drawn up on the
dock to receive the royal ambassadors home, and there
was such complete mystification in their little faces
because there had to be so much official bowing and
ceremonial to be gone through before their parents
could reach them. They came second in the reception;
and it did seem an extremely illogical procedure to
them.

The death of Queen Victoria occurred when prepara-
tions for the Colonial Tour were almost complete.

"I saw her peaceful end," wrote the Queen to a
friend, and "I talked to them [her children] about the

dear Queen, so that they may never forget their great-grandmother."

For a time it was thought that the death of Queen Victoria would change the plans of the tour, for with the accession of King Edward, the Duke of York and Cornwall was now heir apparent to the throne. These objections, however, were ruled aside, and Their Royal Highnesses duly left Portsmouth for Australia, to be present at the opening of the new Commonwealth of Australia which united in a federal parliament the people of New South Wales, Victoria, South Australia, Queensland, Tasmania, and Western Australia.

On March 16th the *Ophir* was played out of Portsmouth Harbour by massed bands from the shore, while the guns from the ships that lay around thundered a last salute. The parting from her children was over for the Queen, "Those dreadful farewells," she wrote to a friend, "that nearly killed me." She arranged their portraits round the royal cabin, "a sweet picture of baby Mary," which is "too nice and looks so pretty on my table"; also pictures of "David" and "Bertie."

From Ceylon the *Ophir* set sail for Singapore and Australia; there had been a halt at Gibraltar, Malta, Aden, before the royal party reached Ceylon, with receptions at each port, presents exchanged, speeches and compliments.

The enthusiasm and kindness of the natives of Ceylon much impressed and warmed the Duchess, and, added to all the delights of the place—its rich romantic scenery, the Buddhist monastery, the representation of the Peraharu procession, an ancient ceremonial survival of old Hindu rites which the party saw—she had for

guide and instructor an intelligent young monk who
dilated to his rapt visitor on the significance of the
various sights and ceremonials.

The monk himself was no little inspired by the
appreciative listener. The Queen is never behind when
there is an opportunity to receive knowledge and instruction, however diffident she herself may be and is to
impart. There are really few experiences that give
her more pleasure than an acute, informed conversation.
She can and does trace some detail of technical information to some stray seaman or engineer she may
chance upon at Cowes, some shop assistant in London,
a gardener at Sandringham or Buckingham Palace, a
gillie in Scotland—the fruits of which show often unexpectedly and, at times, to the confusion of the official
mind.

The Colonial Tour had an importance and emphasis
for Queen Mary over and above the fact that she was
an ambassadress sent from England to the outposts
of the Empire. It represented her first great official
undertaking in which she stood alone by her husband's
side. As there was no one to criticise her, so was there
no one to guide her in whatever difficulty arose. She
stood or fell alone.

It was a first venture; and on it much depended.
Very little was known about her—even less than was
known in England; and the "conflict of emotion" engendered by the circumstances of her first and second
engagements was uppermost in the minds of the colo-
nists before she arrived.

It has been said that when the Duchess of York returned from her Colonial Tour there was observed a

notable change in her demeanour, a quickened sense of
the right of initiative.

Her courtesy, her sympathy, and the accidental advantage of having been preceded by the worst set of
portraits ever produced by a camera, were elements in
the overwhelming success she achieved in the Colonies.
She came, and she conquered.

Queen Mary's zest for travel, her avidity for fresh
sights and other scenes, no less than her capacity to
retain them fixed, enduring in her memory, is a continual source of wonder to those who accompany her
abroad. Her interest is inexhaustible, and only equalled
by her physical and mental power of endurance. She
does not travel well by sea; but in all other respects is
a good traveller. Many have essayed to keep pace with
her ardour on these excursions; mostly they fail.

Her capacity for travel I may best convey perhaps
in a remark she made on board the *Ophir*, on its return
after seven months and a half concentrated, intensive
travel round the world in 1901. It was addressed to
the children's schoolmaster in Sandringham, who accompanied Their Royal Highnesses on the Colonial
Tour; and it should be remembered that, added to the
ordinary fatigues of the travelling, were endless and
protracted official functions wherever the *Ophir*
dropped anchor—from Malta to the Antipodes.

"Travelling," said the beaming traveller, "is too
wonderful. I love it. There is no education in the
world to compare with it!"

There is nothing casual about her travels; to know
one or two things worth knowing in a city or new town,
and to know them thoroughly, is of more joy to her

than any amount of impressionism that leaves little but
bewilderment in its trail.

Places of special interest and attraction to her she
sets out beforehand and, if it is humanly possible, will
beforehand study and read to acquaint herself with
them—an invaluable lesson in travel that Madame
Bricka and her pupil learned in the days of White
Lodge which, with many another lesson absorbed at
that time, is still in use to-day. On the *Ophir* travel
books were always with her to fill the leisure time;
and when she had to set down the book and turn her
hands to other things, it was invariably taken up by
her lady-in-waiting.

With this inborn zest for travel, it may be imagined
with what excitement she looked forward to her visits
to the Dominions overseas. It was a State mission; yet
was it more to her, personally: it was an opportunity
to prove herself.

Gibraltar, Malta, Aden, Ceylon, Singapore they
visited, and after luxuriating in the tropical vegetation
of Ceylon which, she wrote home, "was really wonderful"; and with the memory, a never-to-be-forgotten
memory, of the send-off from Valetta—where, ashore
and on sea, the scene was like a great floating fairyland
—the *Ophir* turned to the route to Australia, going a
little out of its course so that Their Royal Highnesses
might see some of the marvels of the Malay Peninsula.

Four Sultans of the Federated Malay States met the
visitors at Government House, Singapore, and after
lunch the Duchess privately received the wives of the
Perak Sultan and his subordinate chiefs.

Australia at last! "It seems so wonderful to be actually in Australia," the Duchess wrote home to the old country. "It is like a second England, with the same people and the same towns, only the scenery is different. Truly Melbourne is a marvellous city for fifty years' standing. I do not wonder that Australians are proud of their doings."

At Melbourne the reception was more than worthy of a people who could build such a city in fifty years; and with the great accomplishment before her, with a greeting so magnificent, a "set-out" that well rivalled the triumphal arches in the streets of London on her wedding day, the Duchess forgot all her shyness and apprehensions and yielded herself altogether to generous-hearted Australia.

With pomp and ceremony the Commonwealth Parliament was opened; there were military reviews; Labour processions; universities to be visited. The children of the Australian capital passed before Their Royal Highnesses, and from the Minister of Education the Duchess received gifts for her own children at home. At Ballarat, the mining centre, she fastened on her frock, to the accompaniment of lusty cheers, a plain gold brooch given to her by the miners.

From New South Wales, across the intervening stretch of ocean, the *Ophir* went to Auckland, where, following the presentation to the Duchess of a beautiful greenstone casket, was a military review on a scale never before attempted in New Zealand, and the laying of the foundation-stone of the Queen Victoria High School for Maori Girls in which the Duchess of York, it need hardly be said, took tremendous interest.

To the heart of Maoriland they went, where 6,000

Maoris had gathered for the welcoming; and where they met the old guide Sophia, who, in the days before the Tarawere eruption, piloted many a party of tourists. From old Sophia the Duchess elicited much of Maori folklore, and, after receiving the gifts of the native chiefs on the village green, the royal party returned to Auckland, to sail for Wellington.

From Christchurch the party went to Tasmania, saw the tree-felling powers of the Tasmanian bushmen among a hundred and one thrilling sights; and in token of those days on the beautiful island of Hobart, Queen Mary still has a mineral selection of specimens she brought home for the children, and a black opossum rug presented by the ladies of Tasmania.

From Australia the party visited Mauritius, an event which they had anticipated with keen interest, having hitherto learned something of "your beautiful island," as the Duke of York wrote, "rich in honourable traditions in the history of literature and statesmanship; proud of its association with naval achievements that shed equal glory on England and France. . . ."

South Africa as a whole had to be left out of the tour, for the War was still in progress; but the *Ophir* called at Durban, and from Durban the party journeyed to Maritzburg, the seat of government of Natal. Then to Cape Town. Then, skirting the coast of West Africa, they reached the Cape Verde Islands; and thence made a straight course to Quebec.

At Montreal, the commercial capital of the Dominion of Canada, the ladies of the reception committee presented Her Royal Highness with the maple-leaf spray in gold, ornamented with enamel and diamonds, which,

GEORGE AND MARY WITH THEIR FIRST BABY,
AND THE DUKE AND DUCHESS OF TECK

© W. & D. Downey

QUEEN MARY IN HER CORONATION ROBES

at the recent opening of Canada House in London, one or two of the same ladies of the reception committee in Montreal were to see worn by Queen Mary.

The Canadian memory harbours especially two incidents of their first sight of the Duchess of York. One incident relates to the wife of a Canadian clergyman who, rather embarrassed at being presented to Their Royal Highnesses, was advancing towards them with faltering steps; and the swift, instinctive gesture of the Duchess, going out to meet her with both hands outstretched.

The other relates to a hostess who found herself rather tongue-tied and ill at ease with her royal visitors. The Duchess of York, however, seized the first opportunity to ask if she might see the children in the nursery, and added with sudden inspiration: "And may I show you my children's pictures?"

Small wonder that, on their departure from the Dominions, the Duke and Duchess of York were pronounced "the most delightful guests."

Ottawa impressed the Duchess with its magnificent offices and buildings; also an entertainment cleverly devised, which included a representation in facsimile of the life of the lumbermen, descendants of the old French voyageurs, which took place in a neighbouring forest, where, in a shanty erected for the occasion, the visitors partook of pea-soup and pork and beans to complete the "local colour."

It was with a full heart and a grateful one that the Duchess said good-bye to Canada at Halifax, feeling that she had made many friends; and much moved by the affectionate regard of the people. It was surely appropriate that the Queen's first test for great state duties should have taken place in the warm-hearted, cordial Dominions overseas, where values in human relation are more simple and direct, where the people she moved among were best fitted to perceive and to appreciate her sterling qualities and natural diffidence. Always she has kept treasured in her heart the memory of their infinite kindness and warmth at a time when she most needed the assurance and support of these qualities. They saw, and they were conquered; they gave as only a free and generous people can give. In the flood of welcome before their very eyes she expanded and grew more beautiful. No conqueror returned from his victories abroad with a heart more filled with humble thanks.

XIV

QUEEN MARY'S close and vigilant attention to housewifely matters, has been emphasised to tedious lengths; which has tended greatly to obscure and distract from the most salient points of her service in this particular.

It is true that no English Queen has surpassed Queen Mary in jealous guardianship of the royal households which they hold in custody for the Empire; and it is true that many of these royal homes have been neglected and indifferently treated from reign to reign, not infrequently vitiated by bad or mediocre tastes; and often allowed to run riot from sheer incompetence. But Queen Mary's purpose and application in the royal homes is a part of her life and not its paramount interest; a colossal duty, splendidly fulfilled, leavened perhaps by natural taste and inclination.

Affecting pictures have been drawn from time to time in periodicals at home and abroad of Queen Mary conducting a visit to her larders and linen cupboards at Buckingham Palace or Windsor Castle; and this has fostered the popular misapprehensions with regard to the domestic aspect of the Queen's life to such an extent that it becomes necessary to say that she has neither time nor the occasion for such intimacy with the royal larders or linen cupboards; that though she may be precisely aware of the condition of affairs prevailing there, it does not come from personal contact.

What Queen Mary would be like given a suburban house and sole conduct of it, is not difficult to imagine; for at Holyrood has been seen her readiness to tuck up her sleeves and attack furniture and carpets; and when Sir Charles Kenderdine, the creator of Roehampton Hospital for limbless soldiers, once called at Buckingham Palace in response to the Queen's command, he found Her Majesty hanging pictures with the greatest of gusto. The ladies who wait on the Queen have, from time to time, seen her walk into a servant's room and, finding the pictures indifferently set out, rearrange them "with the same care as if it had been her own sitting-room." These occasional excursions in actual domesticity have left no doubt in the minds of those who witnessed them that Queen Mary would not be discomposed by or unable personally to conduct a small house in suburbia. It is simply that she is capable of these things, rather than burdened with an appetite for them; as indeed are most women, and above all things Queen Mary is a woman.

There is a story told by a prominent Labour M.P. whose wife visited Queen Mary at Buckingham Palace in company with the wife of another Labour M.P. The entire unaffectedness of Queen Mary, the remarkable ease with which the conversation flowed along the lives of husbands, wives, children, homes, and such other subjects as relate intimately to the lives of mothers, called from them the loudest of praises. As they passed out through the gates of Buckingham Palace the final encomium was delivered, to the satisfaction of both:

"And I'll guarantee that if we went in her kitchen, it would be as clean as ours."

To realise and to appreciate the real domestic service and accomplishments of Queen Mary, there must first be realised, however inadequately, what composes the royal homes. Consider, for example, Windsor Castle— its splendour and magnificence, its vastness, and the national treasures alone contained in this majestic place, more regal than the palace of any king—this tangible witness to the whole of English history, as well as fortress and ecclesiastical college and home of the English monarchs since Edward the Confessor had a palace at Old Windsor which he bequeathed to the Abbey at Westminster.

Windsor Castle is *one* of the royal homes for which Queen Mary is domestically responsible to the nation, whose possession it is. At Windsor, they speak of Queen Mary as the "Master Mind"; which title she wears for her so-called "domestic" accomplishments there.

Setting aside the State Apartments, the chapels, the parks, the picture galleries, the armoury, the keeps and towers, the treasures of Windsor and its separate architectural memorials to so many English Kings and Queens of the past; the library, the gateways—all of which things are known as Windsor Castle to the public visitor—there are, in the Upper Ward of the Castle, in the various residential towers in Middle and Lower Wards, alone, one thousand odd rooms not seen by the

visitor, as also are not seen the royal suites used by
the King and Queen when they are in residence.

Domestic!   It is such a ludicrously inadequate word
to apply to the work of Queen Mary in the royal homes
—in Buckingham Palace, Balmoral, Holyrood, as well
as Windsor Castle—of which she is no less than custodian, and as the Marquis of Crewe said to me on an
occasion, "Her Majesty likes to feel that she is custodian for the nation."   The knowledge of this also is
her reward.

Truly the industry of Queen Mary in the royal
homes, her downright thoroughness, the capacious range
of her mind, its varied and ceaseless activity in orderly
progression, would burden and oppress the imagination
were it not transmuted by her utter selflessness, her
watchword: I Serve!

It was an acute saying of the late Lady Katharine
Coke, who served the Queen's mother long and well,
and was in waiting with Her Majesty until she was past
eighty, when a new and younger lady-in-waiting once
expressed her bewilderment at the soundness of Queen
Mary's judgment on whatever it was brought to bear,
especially in relation to some delicate, personal problem.

"It bewildered me, too," said Lady Katharine Coke,
"until I realised that it was always sound because nothing of Self is ever allowed to enter into her judgments."

Because there is nothing of self in it, Queen Mary's
service to the nation in the custodianship of the royal
homes is so magnificent, so effective.   It halts one
instinctively on the threshold of her life to shed the
last remnant of frivolous curiosity and that miscellany
of impertinences which the most scrupulous patriot does

not blush to entertain for royalty. It compels reverence; it engenders profound respect where reverence,
perhaps, is hardly possible.

In Buckingham Palace it is an axiom: "There are
no slaves here; only the King and Queen: they are
slaves to duty."

When one looks at the fruits of Queen Mary's domestic duties, her sleepless service in the royal homes,
now apparent, and those that can be appreciated only
by generations to come who shall walk through Windsor Castle and marvel at the memory of this incomparable custodian of the wealth and glory of a great
Empire, well might one pray: Would that I were such
a slave!

The machinery of the royal homes is mercifully
organised so that it may work in spite of the royal
occupant. This is a fact to grasp in the effort to understand and appreciate Queen Mary's domestic service
to the nation; for one need hardly emphasise how very
indifferently the machinery works when there is no
incentive from the top, from the head of the house;
when there is no one much to care; or with the capacity
for caring.

It is much in the caring; Queen Mary cares—tremendously. Balance—Harmony—Order. These are
her domestic principles. A disorderly room, like a
disorderly life, frets her very soul; it is abhorrent to
her. To find herself in an impossible room, loaded
with impossible furniture—however ancient, full of
associations and priceless in money value—that is slipshod and unequally placed in a confusion of Periods,
discomposes her mind far more even than the sight

of ivy playing havoc with the sanitary appurtenances
of a house—her particular aversion. ("How my fingers tingle for a pair of clippers," she murmured one
day on the Sandringham estate, eyes sparkling in an-
ticipation, as she surveyed an especially luscious growth
of ivy wreaking beautiful devastation on the walls and
pipes of the house. The clippers, however, were not
forthcoming.)

It is unfortunately true that royal homes are nearly
always in danger of becoming merely a collection of
things, a medley of pricelessness, without the caring,
unresting mind to infuse order, individuality. With
the advent of King Edward to the throne Windsor
Castle was a painful example of this melancholy fact.
King Edward, with the valued help of advisers like
Sir Guy Laking, began the good work of calling order
from chaos: pictures and other treasures were unearthed
from dark cellars and obscure corners, and reassembled;
advice was sought and gratefully received on all manner of domestic and decorative problems created by
and left over from the long, preceding reign. The
process of resolving some degree of order in the confusion was slow and laborious, and inevitably the task
left to Queen Mary enough work to appal and intimidate a less resolute spirit.

Her Majesty, with characteristic modesty, speaks of
having "simply continued" the work of King Edward;
and it is interesting to know that her training to become
the authority on pictures, furniture, heraldry, the expert in antiques that she is to-day, only began at the
death of King Edward, when came her own responsibility for the royal homes.

Her Majesty has said that after her marriage, during her visits to Dresden and other places abroad, she began first to be interested in furniture and antiques; her serious studies, however, only set in when she came to Windsor Castle. Her own early married homes were furnished largely on wedding presents.

How ably she learned after her accession to the throne is written in every room in every royal home, and not without interest is the fact that, often when there is doubt outside about the authenticity of this or the period of the other—a miniature or piece of furniture—it is surreptitiously sent into the Palace for Queen Mary's verdict—which is usually accepted as final.

Domesticity, for itself, leaves her notably cold; relate it to a person, to personality, and she is all eagerness, Lady Joan Verney once told me. It is her reaction to the castle and to the cottage; it is not the object in itself that appeals, so much as the personal associations connected with the object.

Supplementing, and greatly augmenting, the Queen's natural gifts for guardianship, her talents for managing vast households, and turning them into homes from vast repositories of souvenirs and priceless historical treasures, goes long and profound study into the past and into the present on furniture, china, tapestries— every single subject that will make her a more knowing and excellent custodian.

She is a genealogical expert; she is an authority on Georgian times; on the periods of furniture, the niceties of china, rare and otherwise, she is informed to the finger-tips, and "has a power for extracting from books, especially old books, more interesting personal associations, illuminating and invaluable scraps of knowledge than anyone I have known," I was told one day in the china pantries adjoining the royal kitchens at Windsor by the late Inspector of the Castle, who should know after the numberless years of his service.

Which led us to yet another story of Queen Mary's passion to KNOW about the possessions in the royal homes, "For then they become somehow so much more interesting," she says.

The story relates to the china pantries, and a certain dinner-service decorated with Greek and Etruscan figures and models in chocolate colour on a background of red, with black borders—one of the gems of the royal china collection.

The origin of the dinner-set had been recorded; but the record, to Queen Mary's distress, had either been lost or mislaid. It was known, however, that the set had been presented to George III by the King of the Two Sicilies. One day, in a flutter of excitement, the Queen announced: "I was reading Fanny Burney the other day in London, and found that she mentions a dinner-set given to King George III.

"How I wish we could find out if this is the dinner-set of which we can find no record."

From this start, the search began. It was conducted with all the eagerness, enthusiasm, and determination which Queen Mary's lightest wish can engender in her servants. This, however, was more than a mere wish!

From Windsor the search spread to London and the British Museum, where, in the remotest archives of that place, the whole history of the dinner-set was unearthed!

What joy! Ecstasy! It transpired that George III had presented two bronze cannon to the King of the two Sicilies for his yacht; which had so greatly pleased King Ferdinand that he had ordered the dinner-service to be made in the royal potteries and copied from Greek and Etruscan models. They were duly presented to George III in 1787. The discovery in the British Museum contained, too, much interesting and curious lore relating to the royal potteries where the dinner-set was made, the Greek and Etruscan prototypes, and other circumstances of the gift. And, at least on that day, there was more joy in the royal bosom over one dinner-set, tabulated at last, than over the ninety-nine other china relics with prim, perfected histories.

The domestic genius of Queen Mary is especially to be noted in its relation with her domestics—the innumerable officials, servants, the hosts of the households, all of whom she conspicuously leaves to their own particular work. Intrusion, encroachment, would be unthinkable, because unnecessary and an absurd waste of time; and Queen Mary does not waste time in her household affairs.

For what are her servants there if not to do their own work? It is curious, the facility she has for knowing about things without ever intruding; for being keenly aware and immensely appreciative about everything that is done for her; yet seems always far off, in the distance.

It matters tremendously to her if work is done well —a room well arranged, a garden attractive—work that shows in the fruits that it was more than perfunctory; that caring went with the doing.

Are they not also custodians for the nation?   Are we not one in this great service?

This is the spirit of the royal households; and what most strikes a looker-on is the facility of the royal mistress and her so great capacity for personally identifying herself with her countless servants, in the ramification of their services.   This, and this alone, is why her servants, to the lowest, work so devotedly; and so precious little slips her observation.

Of course the Queen will see and know!   Unconsciously her eyes, all-seeing, range over a room.   She has the trained mental habit of concentration, close observation—the habit that serves the country so well when she deals with persons, and is called upon to consider small matters and great that will in some way affect the Empire.

With the Queen this compassing glance is habitual; but I am informed of at least one occasion when she was entirely out-glanced by King George.   It occurred at Sandringham.   The King and Queen had interrupted their walk to call informally on an official of the estate about some matter relating to the business of the estate.   They had hardly been shown into the drawing-room (which had recently been repapered with a creamy surface) when the King observed to the lady of the house, wife of the estate agent, what a pity it was that her walls should have been spoiled with a blot, and, simply courteous as ever, enquired if he could not send down some paint to cover it!

The blot had occurred in a remote, inconspicuous

corner of the room, and was to all casual appearance, entirely obscured by the writing bureau. It had been splashed in the filling of a fountain-pen—and no one before had even noticed it.

.   .   .   .   .   .

It is impossible to convey adequately how much Queen Mary had accomplished in the royal castles and palaces. A recitation of the facts would fill a library, cloud the imagination, and, no doubt, succeed in concealing the most vital elements of her service.

Her Majesty has little of the personal, possessive instinct; but she is justly proud and intensely jealous of the great possessions of the Empire entrusted to her care. In guarding and caring for these possessions, in increasing their numbers and preserving their value, she is relentless of her own time and work, and exacting in her demands of others appointed to help her in this great work. No one more nobly fulfils a nation's trust. She leaves nothing to luck, or the mood of some workman, artist, or official commissioned to carry out some repair, or recreation. No detail is too small to engage her interest or command her intelligence. Detail matters, as does the whole.

In the domestic domain her rigour is felt. Here she exacts the best; and gives always of her own best to measure overflowing. You may not trifle with a possession of the nation!

Of the infinite trouble she will take, the close attention to detail she will pay to achieve perfection, many stories are current. For example, there were to be fresh hangings and tapestries in the Blue Room at

Windsor Castle. To blend the shades of the blue harmoniously was no easy matter, now would such precision be essential but to the eye of an artist or a
connoisseur of colour schemes in interior decoration.
It was found necessary to observe the effects in half-
lights. To induce the dark by shrouding out the light
from the window was not to get the exquisite exactness
of the darkening evening. "We will wait for the night
and I will come down," said the Queen—and came,
in a few fleeting moments snatched at a crowded time,
just immediately before dinner.

"Incidentally, I shall not forget," said the veteran
servant of the Castle whose responsibility the room
happened to be, "how amazingly beautiful the Queen
looked with her sapphires on an old gold dinner frock,
the badge of the Garter on her arm. Her presence lit
up the blue room. I held my breath at the strange and
so entirely unexpected vision."

The colours of the room inharmoniously blended,
like a careless or inaccurate history appended to some
treasure in Windsor, offends greatly her sense of perfection. It is so extraordinary how, unconsciously
almost, she assembles parts to a whole and relates the
seemingly diverse—by an intuition, a sort of unconscious observation.

It just happens that, under her vigilance, separate
pieces find their place. The story of the china set of
George III, Queen Charlotte and their children, reproduced in biscuit china, is typical. This quaint ornament I saw standing complete on the Queen's sitting-
room table at Windsor Castle; but it was never
complete until Queen Mary came to Windsor, and no

one knows how long it remained incomplete; or that
anyone much cared.

The story is this: In the Grand Corridor of Windsor which leads to the drawing-rooms of the private and
royal suites there hung for many years a picture by
Zoffany of King George III, Queen Charlotte, and
their children. Some of the children in Zoffany's picture are presented close to Queen Charlotte; four others
are depicted in the distance playing cockatoo. It was
known that in the royal china collection there had been
for many years a biscuit china reproduction of Queen
Charlotte and some of the children near her; and
then suddenly one day Queen Mary came upon a
corresponding reproduction of George III—in biscuit
china.

Instantly she assumed that somewhere were the
missing children and the cockatoo; and there had once
been a complete biscuit china reproduction of Zoffany's
picture in the Grand Corridor.

Enquiries were set on foot; art dealers apprised of
the missing link; the children and the cockatoo were
ultimately traced and purchased, at the Queen's bidding
—which is the story of the complete biscuit china set
in Her Majesty's sitting-room.

No doubt it is this sense of perfection which explains
her capacity for observing small variations in objects
far beyond that of most persons. The smallest, slightest variations in objects—in furniture, china, picture
frames, carpets, panellings and so on—she sights
instantly.

The chairs, for example: these were generally made
for the royal homes in half-dozens or dozens. One

half-dozen would arrive perfect to the minutest detail; the next batch might be guilty of small variations in the details of their flowers, cupids, turned or plain stretchers.

In course of time these dozens and half-dozens are inadvertently separated and scattered in various rooms of the various residences in Scotland, Norfolk, Windsor, London. So slight are these variations that no one notices them—except the Queen, who has a habit of walking into a room and commenting quietly to this Inspector of the Castle and the other that here is a chair which surely belongs to the set in a certain wing of Windsor—or London; so that, after long intervals, the "strays" find their way back to their proper set.

For the ladies of the Court, too, it is a common experience to watch Queen Mary pounce on a chair in Holyrood or Windsor, and announce triumphantly: "And here is the chair we have been looking for to complete the set" in such a place. It is an incident; but a common incident in the experiences of the Queen's ladies-in-waiting.

The observance of small variations is even more valuable in china, where the differences may indicate "first" and "second" qualities; for the cheaper "seconds" are often distinguished by their deficiency in some tiny ornament—a small flower, or insect.

The royal homes are always with their royal mistress. She has a zest for antique shops; but she has a purpose with them, too. Her eye lights on a gem: "How admirably that will do for so and so!" In another object are possibilities for somewhere else. Wherever she goes, there is the same awareness that perhaps she will light on a treasure for Windsor; an adornment for Buckingham Palace, an indispensable piece of furniture for Holyrood or Balmoral. "Just the thing!"

Room after room one goes through in London, Windsor, Norfolk, Scotland, and everywhere is evidence of her tremendous concern. Here is a room of the royal library at Windsor; set out under glass are the christening clothes, looking rather faded and a little jaundiced by time, worn by George IV, with little mits and cuffs to match. "The Queen acquired them recently at a sale."

Or again one halts before an unusually rich and beautiful hanging.

"That was in a drawer in —— for twenty-odd years! The Queen had it taken out, cleaned, and hung."

One stops before a picture. "The Queen bought it at —— galleries."

The catalogue of her purchases is endless; but there is no reckless extravagance in the buying. On the contrary: the sagacity displayed in many of these purchases would incite envy in many—more especially when the money is forthcoming not from her own private purse. So often, however, it is from her own purse that the nation's treasures are enriched.

It is necessary to wander in those parts of Windsor Castle that are not shown to the public, most acutely to realise and to appreciate Queen Mary's domestic achievements. I am assured by those who should know, whose duties relate to the care and constant guarding of the countless treasures in Windsor, that there is not

an object, from the most rare to that of least account,
with which Her Majesty is not familiar.

She is the Perfect Guide to Windsor!

As one walks along the magnificent Grand Corridor,
on to which most of the private suites open, and looks
up and down, round and about at the innumerable
pictures and treasures ranging variously from General
Gordon's Bible, presented to Queen Victoria by Miss
Gordon, to that breathlessly beautiful carved ebony
cabinet of Flemish workmanship, presented to Charles
II by Louis XIV of France, with its drawers consummately inlaid and signed by the various masters
who carved them—at the paintings of Zoffany, Reynolds, Gainsborough; the innumerable miniatures, panellings, tapestries, statuary—it is almost overwhelming
to realise how much of caring, study, observation and
reading has gone to make the Perfect Guide.

And this knowledge, this expertness and authority
Queen Mary wears so easily, conceals so modestly.
Now and then, perhaps, a guest, wandering with Their
Majesties through some part of the Castle, may pause,
note and wonder, at the frequency of King George's
laughing:

"May: now you know all about this."

Where she does not know, she finds out; and where
perhaps it is not possible to find out, she awaits the
publication of some new diaries which, perhaps, contain
some passing reference to one of the many treasures
in the royal homes.

When the Faringdon *Diaries* were published recently
she put them to excellent use. She is familiar with all
the Georgian diarists; and from them has gained much

that has contributed to histories of relics that were inadequate or inaccurate; or supplied the entire history. Now there is light on some miniature that has long lain without its history; or again some choice piece of furniture finds its historic or personal connotation. Every channel is tapped; for information, enlightenment, it is well known, may come in conversation with some visitor; or when travelling abroad. It matters not whence comes the light.

Added to Queen Mary's extraordinary power of observation is another formidable gift referred to in enlightened court circles as her "uncanny memory." She has this "uncanny memory" especially for persons; but it is not limited to faces and persons. It operates elsewhere and in other matters; and the knowledge of it helps the better to understand her well-nigh superhuman accomplishments in the royal homes.

One day during a tour of Windsor with an official of the Office of Works, the Queen suddenly halted and remarked: "Curious, and I think it must have been years ago; but I distinctly remember somewhere, in this part of the Castle, when I was Princess of Wales, you took me in a room and showed me some tapestry. I have never seen it since. I remember the room was rather dark, and I am sure you took the tapestry from a bottom drawer."

The official racked his brain, cogitated long and painfully; but he could remember nothing. Later that day he referred the matter to his colleagues. One of them had a specially long memory, and "specialised in remembering" (a valuable asset now in this side of the royal service).

The Queen had given a description of the tapestry which, apparently, she had seen for a few fleeting moments "years ago." It had all "come back to her"— the circumstances—and the texture of the tapestry.

For weeks they cogitated, and finally came to the unanimous conclusion that here, at least, Her Majesty must be mistaken! And concealed, as best they could, their pleasure in this solution of the problem.

Alas! for six months later the tapestry came to light —from the obscure depths of some drawer in a room in St. James's Palace. With the object now before them, the Office of Works recalled the "darkened room, the bottom drawer" where "years ago" it had actually used to reside at Windsor Castle.

It is rather in connection with persons that Queen Mary's memory has been described as "uncanny." She simply does not forget faces. In a passing crowd in far-off Tasmania, in the turmoil and distraction of a "State Drive," Queen Mary observed to her lady-in-waiting of a man in the swarming crowds: "There is ——. I heard him preach once when I was a child; he was curate in East Sheen."

Enquiries subsequently proved that it was ——, the curate of East Sheen!

In India again: "Usually Her Majesty was apprised beforehand of the people about to be met; but on at least two occasions, noted by the staff, she recognised persons, one of whom she had met once in Canada, years ago; the other an officer who two years previously had been on the guard of honour at Ballater."

One day the Queen was visiting a Home in Richmond where she recognised an old man working in the garden.

"I am glad to see you again," she said, putting out her hand. "Don't you remember how, when we were children, we used to climb into your garden cart?"

"I remember when I was at Stuttgart with the Queen," Lady Mary Trefusis has told me, "and we stopped before two miniatures.

" 'Why,' said the Queen, "there is a reference to them in ———. I remember reading it with Bricka at White Lodge!' "

As Lady Mary concluded, "It must have been twenty years since she had read it!"

.   .   .   .   .   .

There is immense conservative force in Queen Mary, and little of the purely creative; and this conservatism is seriously allied to a zest for Progress.

The paradox, showing as it does so much in her work, shows also in her personal attitude, her unexpected point of view.

For example: she is unexcelled in her Victorian reverence for age; and yet has a passion for Youth—trusts it, believes in it, selects it fearlessly.

In domestic matters the paradoxical attitude shows most in the eagerness with which she will seize hold and adopt the most up-to-date labour-saving device. Queen Mary, as is well known, is no amateur at an exhibition of labour-saving devices. She enthusiastically adopts them in her own homes, even though they were not recognised in the reign of Queen Anne.

Her mind is flexible; so, too, are her fingers. She herself designed the adornments of an exquisite writing-table I saw in the Chinese Room at Windsor Castle;

and was the first to see, so I was assured, the possibilities in the mandarin cloaks presented by some Oriental potentate to Queen Victoria, that had long mouldered in dusty obscurity and now do excellent service in the Chinese Room as hangings and settee covers.

Nor does her inventiveness cease with matters of adornment—decoration. All the plans of the cottages to be erected on the royal estates first pass her vigilant eye before they are realised in bricks and mortar.

Her survey of the plans is characteristically conducted in terms of the convenience of the woman who, as Queen Mary well knows, will probably have to spend most of her life in the cottage.

This copper must be removed from the interior of the house to the outside; for why, Her Majesty would argue, should any woman's home be filled with steam on washing days, which are unpleasant enough, in all conscience, without the additional irritant of steam that with the evening will leave the whole house damp and uncomfortable?

Again: the pantry must be moved nearer the kitchen; for why should a tired woman waste steps going to and from her kitchen and pantry?

The same care, the same great patience and understanding, is brought to bear on a cottage going up at Balmoral or Sandringham as if it were an additional wing to Buckingham Palace or Windsor.

Nowhere does her consideration fail; nowhere does her interest flag. Always she is so mightily human. The lives and circumstances of her servants are as familiar to her as the lives and circumstances of her courtiers and ladies. Her cottagers must have comfort as her ladies must have consideration; their humanity is their claim; and there are no degrees in these matters.

A report is brought to the Palace that Lady Eva Dugdale is stricken with a sudden illness.

"My poor, poor Eva!"

It is nearly midnight; and Queen Mary is hurrying post-haste a score and more miles out of London to get to the bedside.

Or is it a servant in disgrace, and about to be discharged from the royal household?

"But," says Queen Mary, "do your realise that you are turning him on the world without a single hope— without a chance to get other work? You say he is to have no 'character.' "

The "powers" are adamant: things are done in this way.

And officially Her Majesty, Queen Mary, must bow to the inevitable—officially.

In private, however, she swiftly becomes active. She summons a friend to her aid—one who can and will give the man a chance; "stand by" him in a new job; encourage him; remove possible temptation "until he is strong enough to stand alone again."

This is the woman that is Queen Mary.

.   .   .   .   .   .

Beauty in order and harmony.

This is Queen Mary's domestic method, the principle on which the royal homes are laid out. By the studied, rigorous application of this principle the private suites at Windsor Castle, like the State Apartments, with their emblems of the past, are rescued from being mere show places—a confusion of beautiful things with the beauty lost in utter disorder.

To begin with an empty house and furnish it with things of beauty would be an enviable task compared with the task of the royal custodian who must create beauty out of what already exists in overwhelming profusion.

"It was Queen Mary who taught me the art of 'balancing' a room," I was once told at Windsor by an official who had long been concerned with the carpets, furniture, and china of the Castle—one who had served Queen Victoria and Queen Alexandra.

"The Queen's sense of balance is perfect, and, of course, incommunicable; but one learns from her some of the rudiments of balance.

"The moment she walks into a room she feels what is wrong or, rather, that needs rearranging to achieve perfection, as far as perfection is possible. It may be a picture she suggests moving to another place—a piece of the furniture, the china—even the flowers—something quite slight which yet achieves magical results.

" 'But don't you see,' she will say, 'how much better this looks here?' "

It is the same everywhere—at Holyrood, Windsor, Buckingham Palace, York Cottage, there are always stories of Queen Mary "balancing" a room.

"I was with the Queen one day at Holyrood," Lady Bertha Dawkins has told me. "We had hardly got inside the door when Her Majesty said: 'Now I see! Of course, it's that candelabra!'

"The candelabra was removed to the room she indicated, fitting into the scheme of things as though it had been designed specially for the purpose; while the room from which it had been moved was left perfect."

The touch of Queen Mary is everywhere evident. In her own private suite at Windsor her "eighteenth-century taste," as Lady Joan Verney once described it, is perhaps given more rein: in her sitting-room, with its cream and gold walls, soft rose-coloured hangings; the Georgian relics for which she has an especial fondness collected about her; the large, handsome painting of Queen Charlotte and the Princess Royal by Cotes; the Duchess of Cambridge, her grandmother; a Gainsborough of the Duke and Duchess of Cumberland; Princess Sophia of Gloucester by Reynolds—an exquisite child picture. There is that large spaciousness in the furniture: in the magnificent Reisener commode, with two companion *encoigneurs*; the Boule cabinet and various other pieces of exquisite French work; the writing-table, inlaid Boule, at which she sits to write her letters, on which are crowded miniatures and photographs of her family and friends; the clock and vases of Derbyshire spar,—it is all precise and orderly, saved from a too severe exactness by giant bowls of flowers filled from the royal gardens usually with pale pink carnations, these being among her favourite flowers.

The precision of the writing-table is very characteristic: stationery sorted and placed, memorandum pad unruffled at her elbow; and no signs apparent of the systematic industry which it ceaselessly witnesses when the Court is in residence.

Colour she has always with her, everywhere. Her

"atmosphere" is conspicuously lacking the sombre; black is her particular aversion.

Everywhere in Windsor, to the ante-room of the State Apartments, Queen Mary radiates balance, order, harmony; and Windsor was greatly in need of these qualities. It is known that, so great was the influence of Queen Victoria through her own reign, had there been in her time a piece of Sheraton placed in the centre of a Jacobean room, it would have been felt a sort of irreverence to have moved it to a more congruous setting—to a Sheraton room. Suitability was never consulted; the march of time, making what once was appropriate in furnishings now ludicrous, left Windsor notably untouched: not a piece of bric-à-brac was moved; and more things were justified for the memory of Queen Victoria than Sheraton and Chippendale in a room that was intended to represent the French period.

King Edward altered much; Queen Mary continued his work in a stringent manner. Thus has been achieved the perfection that now prevails.

No one more reverences the memory of Queen Victoria than does Queen Mary; and reverently, with terrible thoroughness, Windsor was reborn in beauty and order. The methods of the household, too, were brought into some relation with the times.

Nor was attention confined to the interior of Windsor Castle. It should be known that the shrubs and trees in the "Slopes" (on the north side of the Castle) owe much of their freshness and many of their improvements to the care of Queen Mary. In days past they presented simply a dense, tangled wilderness.

The weedy undergrowth is now cleared away, and the trees of the "Slopes" are clear, open, independent, and vigorous.

Forest trees have a great charm and attraction for the Queen; and inevitably the Windsor Great Park and Forest did not escape her vigilance. Faithfully she attends the removal of decayed trees and the replanting of young ones. The "Queen Adelaide" tree, which stands, as does "Queen Mary's" tree, at a rare look-out spot on the brow of a hill three miles from the Castle, had long been left in decay—to the danger of passers-by. Last year, at Her Majesty's direction, it was re-planted with a young beech.

Order out of Chaos—Law and Harmony—they are inseparable from the presence of the Queen. To the Ministerial Suite of the Grand Corridor you trace it— in the engravings of English Prime Ministers past and gone, collected in this one place instead of being distributed at random over the Castle.

To the archives of the souvenirs this same law and order prevails. I have seen neat little bound notebooks in the library at Windsor in which Queen Mary enters the history and circumstances, not only of her own treasured "stuff," but that of King George's and Queen Victoria's rich and varied possessions.

This organisation of precious trivialities is wonderfully complete in Queen Victoria's collection, where much of the "stuff" has no title to be treasured in a place so full of treasures as Windsor Castle. Aside, however, from the Queen's immense veneration for Queen Victoria, she is a great harbourer of sentiment, especially the sentiment of the past. At Buckingham

Palace are the same souvenir entry books; at Balmoral, too; and one cannot but think of the generations to come who will greatly bless this custodian, so jealous of the past, so careful of the present; learning so much from her own queenship, and saving them endless searchings and fatigues.

There is so little that is perfunctory about Queen Mary, even to the acceptance of gifts, great or small. One is reminded of this by an incident which happened at the recent opening of the new Canada House.

Assembled in the lobby of the building at the opening were many Britishers, English and Canadian, intimately associated with the Dominion. To the incredulous surprise of the ladies, they noted, instantly the Queen arrived, that she was wearing a small maple spray set with precious stones, that had been given to her by the ladies of Canada when she visited the Dominion as Duchess of York, twenty-four years before.

Nor was this all. Among the ladies assembled was the widow of a distinguished magnate associated with the Canadian railways.

Immediately she saw that Queen Mary was carrying a parasol that her husband had given Her Majesty so many years ago that she herself could not recall the date.

Concluding the incident, the lady in question, who has known Queen Mary all her life, said to me, deeply moved: "There is the graciousness of Queen Mary!"

She had assumed, as all who know Queen Mary would instantly have assumed, that, being shown the list of ladies to be presented at the opening, the thought would naturally occur to Her Majesty that the widow would take pleasure in the sight of the parasol, put to that appropriate use.

That appreciativeness of Queen Mary, combined with her incurable habit of somehow withdrawing when the bouquets are handed round, you may catch in the delightful gestures of her servants and their easy assumption of honourable partnership in the perfecting of the royal palaces. Hers is the inspiration; theirs the fulfilment; and the result is altogether proper and delightful.

In the Wedgwood Room adjoining the private royal suite at Windsor Castle, for example, that precious light of the Queen's eye, so consummately arranged, so altogether delightful, and of her own creating, one is told:

"Lord Curzon gave me the carpet, and WE think it finishes the room. . . ."

And again in the Wedgwood Room: "Oh, WE made it from the smallest beginnings. It started with a plaque in the mantelpiece, which was there when WE came."

One day the Queen remarked that it was a pity all the Wedgwood relics were so distributed about the palaces; they would set each other off to such advantage collected in the same room.

"It was then WE began the search; and you see what WE have made!"

Where one looks for the perfunctory, the menial, or, at worst, the obsequious, one finds the eminently self-respecting servant with much of the infectious dignity of his royal mistress; and it is somehow a rare compliment to the mistress.

After lovingly handling and stroking the Wedgwood panels, let into the backs of the chairs, smoothing an imperceptible crease out of the blue carpet, and a last, long look on the room of OUR creating, we adjourn to some other gem of OUR custodianship.

To the Audience Chamber of cedar-wood, with its walls plastered with exquisite miniatures, the work of the Prince Consort, as the inscription on the door tells: a small, seemingly excessively high room, too precious, perhaps, for the enjoying; a show-room in the least painful sense of the word.

Here we do not linger long: for OUR hand is nowhere to be seen or felt; except in the rare care that is taken of the room to preserve its pristine freshness and artistry; for "WE always leave well alone!"

It is the same in the Royal Library at Windsor, situated at the west end of the State Apartments, and overlooking the North Terrace, which again bears witness to the Queen's unceasing acquirements; and where daily the collection of volumes is enriched.

To be loosed in this wonderful collection of old and valuable works on history, geography, topography, with others of the classical writers, and early printed works (which include a superb copy of the METZ PSALTER, a Caxton on vellum, Charles I's own copy of Shakespeare, Mozart's first Oratorio, a letter of indulgence from Leo X, and papyri from Herculaneum) is to be moved to humble thankfulness for Queen Mary and her unresting care and her awareness of their value.

In the library there reposes one of the richest and

most extensive collections of prints in the whole country, including the Raphael Collection, formed by the Prince Consort, together with 20,000 odd drawings of the old masters. One can rest more than content in their custodian.

Here again one hears the eternal testimonies to Her Majesty's knowledge and concern. It is the same story: "She knows about things; she cares."

Here, between stories of the Queen's zest for French —Georgian—and modern memoirs (in good and ill repute) which are put within easy reach of her when the Court is in residence—and her marked indifference to ephemeral literature—one hears stories of the "uncanny memory" which will suddenly prompt her to enquire for a book added so many years ago to the collection that everyone else has forgotten it.

Far more than by these things, however, is one impressed by the attitude toward the royal mistress of all who serve her.

Royalty does not command this respect, this so great devotion: it is the woman that is Queen Mary.

The innate genuineness of the Queen makes it impossible to flatter her, precisely as it has always saved her from the use of incense and the honeyed word.

Yet what flattery is in the devotion, the quality of the service she compels!

There is no trifling with this mistress; and none know it better than her servants—from the lowest region of the kitchen to those who sit with her in the drawing-room—her ladies. None know better her quiet resolve when it is decreed that certain things are to move. And it is so.

There are those who to-day well remember the piquant incident between Queen Mary and some high household official at Windsor, when Her Majesty enquired about the stories of the Castle.

"Ah, Ma'am; but these places are sacred from us. It has always been so. . . . Even I have never been admitted."

"Really? But I will go." She went.

And there was more surprise in the lower regions of the Castle that day than if the two armoured horsemen, James I and Charles I, seated with tilting lances at rest on the upper landing of the Grand Entrance to the Grand Hall, had come suddenly to life and clattered down the wide stairway.

.   .   .   .   .   .

Cut off as Her Majesty is from the larger world, the unrestrained air outside of palaces, where men and women move and are moved freely without the restraints, severities, and inhibitions imposed by royal etiquette, yet has she a sagacity which, sharpened by her own vivid sensitiveness, tempered by her great humanity, serves her well in the place of actual contact, and alone gives her that acute, capacious understanding which is hers.

Is there a difficulty, is there a distress, is there a delicate situation to be handled inside or outside of her own household? It is to the Queen that they go direct.

It is with a feeling akin to awe that one sees the fruits of Queen Mary's work in Windsor, the stateliest of the royal homes of the Kings of England. It is the same elsewhere, especially in Scotland, where, under Her Majesty's personal guidance, superintendence, and inspiration the interior of the High Commissioner's quarters at Holyrood have been metamorphosed. To and from Scotland the couriers and emissaries of Queen Mary journey—with some new suggestion, some scheme that has occurred to the unresting mind in London or Windsor. Whenever Her Majesty is in Scotland she is continually making private journeys to Holyrood to watch the process of transformation or the effects of her latest scheme there realised.

Yet it is not only the emotion of admiration that one brings away as a lasting memory; it is not the "Master Mind" on which one dwells most in reflection; but her capacity to infuse into the most radical, the most massive project so much of human kindness and understanding; the love and devotion she compels from her servants, rather than the miracle of some feat in interior decoration.

The rebukes that come to these servants for some remissness or stupidity—Queen Mary has a considerable impatience with incompetents—are soon forgotten; for as the late Mlle. Tatry, whose privilege it was to "dress" the Queen when she was a girl at White Lodge, remarked to me once: "I never minded when she flared; for when it passed she was so much the sweeter."

What they do not forget—what remains uppermost in the mind of anyone who has ever known the inner workings of the royal homes—is the humanity and kindness of the royal mistress. Here, one feels, is her "domestic genius."

Never less demonstration went with such deep and

genuine feeling. Always to her servants such boundless understanding. There is a footman who has con-
tracted debts which he is unable to meet; and there is
little immediate hope that he can settle them. His
wife is consumed with anxiety, naturally; and she is
about to become a mother—on the eve of an experience that of itself brings enough worry and anxiety for
one woman.

Queen Mary hears of the circumstances, and pays
the debts; for: "We must really ease her mind; she
has enough to bear at the moment."

One day she is out shopping. Her lady in attendance is lost in admiration of four beautifully tinted,
fragile glasses bought by the Queen during the morning's purchases.

A few days later Her Majesty came into the lady-
in-waiting's room—the tinted glasses in her hand and
that rare smile on her face:

"I saw how you liked them the other day," she said,
handing over the glasses.

The way in which Queen Mary always preserves the
air of "home" wherever she moves in the royal palaces
and castles I cannot better convey than in a story told
to me by Mrs. Clynes. "It was not a big thing," as
Mrs. Clynes remarked, "yet it conveyed so much to
me.

"While I was packing my case to leave Windsor, I
had noticed a kind of bustle and hurry about the housemaid in the corridor. I learned the cause later: she
wanted to be spruce, and cleaned up before the Queen
came round! It was then I learned that always Her
Majesty came in person every morning to see that the

guests' rooms were in due order. And I couldn't help feeling impressed to know that, in spite of all the million and one far greater and more important calls on the Queen's time, especially in the mornings, she yet made time for this courteous little ceremony. She could so easily not have troubled, and found every reason and excuse in the world for not bothering."

XV

THERE is an irony in the fact that it seems to have needed a great war to give to the great woman at Buckingham Palace an opportunity of proving her eminent ability in the political and industrial matters of the nation—to entrust her with situations from which, in normal times, she is rigorously precluded by the very Constitution of the country that proclaims her husband King. And when all has been said of the divine right of the Constitution, the irony remains that the same terrible and tremendous experience which brought her so much of suffering and strain to grey her hair and anguish her heart, brought also to Queen Mary of England a measure of that freedom which is the proud heritage of the least of her husband's subjects.

That she, too, may date her real "coming out" from August 1914 creates yet another bond of understanding between Her Majesty and the women of the British Empire to whom there came strangely, with grief and terror, the open spaces and the unconfined air. She who, at a distance, bound by the robes of majesty, had witnessed the ceaseless struggles of women for what they had called Emancipation was now at liberty to unite with them in one colossal effort for an even greater freedom—the freedom of the Empire.

Their story is her story; one by one from her, too,

the shackles dropped before the grim spectre of war; but if, like a being released suddenly from long confinement, she was momentarily unsteadied by this so great light of the day, there was much to sober her.

Day after day yet another and another contingent of guards marched past Buckingham Palace on their way to France, and a mother no less than a Queen watched them from behind the curtain of an upper window. From the beginning to the end her great heart beat with them: the heart of the mother with two sons serving, and the heart of the Queen. And because there is poignantly blended the ring of them both in the splendid message addressed by Her Majesty to "The Men of Our Army, Navy, and Air Force," I have reproduced it in full:

"I send this message to tell every man how much we, the women of the British Empire at home, watch and pray for you during the long hours of these days of stress and endurance.

"Our pride in you is immeasurable, our hope unbounded, our trust absolute. You are fighting in the cause of Righteousness and Freedom, fighting to defend the children and women of our land from the horrors that have overtaken other countries, fighting for our very existence as a People at Home and Across the Seas. You are offering your all. You hold back nothing, and day by day you show a love so great that no man can have greater.

"We, on our part, send forth, with full hearts and unfaltering will, the lives we hold most dear.

"We too are striving in all ways possible to make the war victorious. I know that I am expressing what is felt by thousands of wives and mothers when I say that we are determined to help one another in keeping your homes ready against your glad home-coming.

"In God's Name we bless you and by His help we too will do our best."

She spoke very little in those early days of 1914; her tears were for the recess of her own room. All that she could DO, her country needed; and had she not always been eminently a woman who could DO things?

.   .   .   .   .   .

Scarcely had war begun in earnest when Queen Mary turned first to put her own house in order. Long before the advent of the Food Controller, and to the consternation of her household, she stopped all luxuries and introduced a system of rationing, beginning with her own self and the King, before asking her servants and household to submit to these rigours.

With vivid clearness (her friends still marvel at it) she foresaw the food shortage in the country and seems to have long anticipated the general system of rationing soon imposed on the whole nation.

"Over and above the vision," I have been told repeatedly, "the Queen acutely felt the horrors and hardships of the soldiers in the trenches, and, at all times deprecating extravagance, even comfort now seemed to her almost criminal."

I must digress a moment to tell a story about King George which excellently conveys the extremely Spartan nature of home life at Buckingham Palace which His Majesty manfully embraced, like the rest of his household, at the Queen's bidding.

© *Campbell Grey*

THE PRINCE OF WALES AND THE PRINCESS MARY,
GARBED FOR THEIR PARENTS' CROWNING

THE KING AND QUEEN IN THE ROBING ROOM,
AFTER OPENING THEIR FIRST PARLIAMENT

It occurred during one of the unending visits which Their Majesties together undertook to the wounded soldiers in hospital. As is well known, hardly a day passed that did not include some hospital visit in the crowded royal schedule. King George was being shown an economical apparatus for heating purposes which suffused an equable heat all over the building:

"But how lucky you are," said His Majesty, rather ruefully. "And you may go from one room to another. You know, we have to live in a corner of one room to keep warm!"

Then, after a moment's deep reflection, His Majesty added:

"And you can have hot baths every day!   I only get a hot bath once a week, now—and—well; you just can't lather soap in cold water, can you?"

Lord Davenport, first Food Controller, and a man not given to extravagant praise, once said to Lady Roxburgh:

"Of all the practical women in this world—my own wife included—there is not a more practical, a more understanding, a more helpful woman than Queen Mary!" This at a time when it was an invidious duty to control the country's food rations.

Lord Davenport talked frequently and freely to Her Majesty during his term as Controller; and found no one more sympathetic, more ready with practical advice.

And here it might seem apt to insert another remark of Queen Mary's when food rationing was about to be imposed.

"Please; I beg of you to see that there is no food

shortage in the East End. We are so much better fitted and equipped to go without than they are."

And she meant what she said!

Before the war was declared, on August 3rd to be precise, Queen Mary summoned her lady-in-waiting from the country by telegram. "Come at once," ran the message. "You may not be able to travel to-morrow."

In the privacy of Queen Mary's room at Buckingham Palace, the lady-in-waiting, Lady Bertha Dawkins, was apprised that war was about to be declared.

"One or two things," Lady Bertha has told me, "remain clearly in my mind about that day: the horror of Her Majesty at the prospect of war, and the resolution in her voice.

" 'All that we women can do for them our soldiers will need,' she said.

"And, 'We must have everything ready. I do not want to have that state of things which prevailed during the Boer War, with everybody just sending what they liked, without relation to the real needs of our soldiers, without organisation.

" 'It entails too much waste, and too great loss of time. Let us strive for central organisations from which to control and direct. Soon, too soon, there will be thousands of women wanting to do something to help and not knowing what to do. Let us be ready for them, too. . . .' "

In point of time, it was not the Central Committee which represented the first great organisation of women to come virtually under the direct leadership of Queen Mary during the early days in August.

Her Majesty was occupied by another great under-taking which I will deal with later, when, on about August 10th, 1914, an industrial situation arose, from out of which, as by a miracle, that exceedingly able body of women known as the Central Committee arose, at the bidding of Queen Mary.

It came to birth in troubled times; it brought Queen Mary her first direct contact with the Labour woman; incident to its career also was the extraordinarily romantic meeting between Queen Mary of England and Mary Macarthur, who, as is known, had spent all her life organising women workers in Trades Unions, and had inspired that considerable organisation known as the "National Federation of the Women Workers of Great Britain."

The story of the Central Committee has never yet been adequately told; it is significant here in that, more than any other of Her Majesty's activities during the War, her relations with the Central Committee most illuminate her gifts in human relationships.

For this reason it has first place in the account of Queen Mary's war service, and, if I emphasise now the personal side of the Central Committee and Her Majesty's associations with it, I do so because it is more relevant to my purpose. It must not be forgotten, however, that the organisation of the Central Committee was as business-like in its workings as it was both able and effective in its fruits.

It is neither more nor less important than any other of Her Majesty's multifarious interests during the War; it is only distinguished by the fact that it best shows Queen Mary's understanding of and sympathy with the women workers, and the power that is hers for compelling respect and devotion from the most diverse people—from those who are the declared enemies of all that the institution of royalty represents.

From those who have nothing to gain and nothing to lose by the friendship of Queen Mary at Buckingham Palace have come the finest tributes to her greatness; it is her "enemies" who say "she is one of the greatest of living Englishwomen." They fixed their eyes on the woman, and in the knowledge only of the woman that is Queen Mary count their gains.

Gains that are theirs yet; even if their gratitude for the inspiration that came with the knowledge of this "new friend" took various and sometimes strange forms when war was over and each went her separate way.

There were those who lay low and said nothing for very fear of putting "The Cause back twenty years"—an irritating, if comprehensible, attitude. There were others who, in the first flush of the new experience, blazoned the woman that was Queen Mary up and down the ranks and lost much thereby for their boldness and their truth; for it is a fact that one tincture of Buckingham Palace is more suspect in certain quarters than a criminal record.

There is something pathetic as well as something very revealing in the picture recently given to me of the late Mary Macarthur sitting up into the night at an hotel in Stourbridge choosing to talk for the most part of her association with Queen Mary. And all the time there would recur, like a Greek chorus, her wistful: "If there should be a revolution! I trust not while I live, for I should have to go and tell the Queen about it."

Mary Macarthur was unburdening to an old friend with whom, as a girl, she had first come to London.

"We began by recounting our lives from that time," the friend has told me. "Then Mary told me from beginning to end her meeting with the Queen, a meeting brought about, I understood, by the Marchioness of Crewe. Mary seemed to want to unburden, and she knew that I was not in the Movement; and she knew that she could unburden freely. It was an anxious night for Mary, the eve of the counting of the votes polled a fortnight earlier by the voters of the Stourbridge division of Worcestershire, for which constituency she had stood at the first General Election where women candidates stood and women voters voted. I remember feeling at the time how deep an impression her association with the Queen had left on her mind that, of all times, she should have then preferred to talk about it. And I shall always remember the words with which she finished her story: 'If there is a great desire in my life, I think it is this: to reveal to the Labour Party the woman that Queen Mary is.'

"And then: 'But could I be her champion? It is more than I dare!'"

. . . . . .

The early days of August 1914 found Queen Mary fully engrossed with the metamorphosis of her Needle-work Guild into a vast central organisation for the control and direction of the voluntary work that women both with and without leisure were doing all over the country.

To the women workers no less than the men workers those early days of war brought trade dislocation, slack time, and unemployment on an unparalleled scale. Countless women over the whole country were thrown into a state of unemployment by the declaration of the moratorium and various other circumstances inevitable to war.

Nor was the plight of the women workers at all improved by the fact that throughout the country women were voluntarily undertaking the making of garments which had before made the employment of regular workers.

Naturally, this circumstance caused much discontent and unrest; while the leaders of the women workers, such as Mary Macarthur, League Secretary of the National Federation of Women Workers, having seen the position she had built up over the years that had gone before crumble round her, now contemplated some form of immediate action to prevent the effect of this voluntary work reacting so disastrously on the women workers to combat this further peril "brought on by the well-meaning and well-to-do, who were seized with a perfect epidemic of needlework and so competed feverishly with unemployed women by the socks, shirts, and garments they turned out for the soldiers," as Miss Gertrude Tuckwell has summed up the case.

The situation was delicate and critical in the extreme. It was brought before the notice of the Workers' War Emergency Committee—a Committee that had been set up by the Labour Party as a whole immediately on the outbreak of war to watch the interests of the workers.

The Workers' War Emergency Committee represented one of the strongest and most influential committees ever formed in the united interests of the Labour Party, with Mr. Henderson as its chairman, who was later succeeded by Mr. Smillie.

Miss Mary Macarthur, in the interests of women workers, also sat on the Committee formed by the Labour Party, and, so urgently was its attention needed to the conditions of women workers that, though the Workers' War Emergency Committee had only held its first meeting on August 10th, by August 13th it was sitting again for the special purpose of considering some action that would prevent the influence of voluntary work from throwing so many women workers out of employment. Queen Mary, as the head of the Needlework Guild, was naturally singled out by the Committee as a possible channel of appeal.

At this meeting of the Workers' War Emergency Committee, August 13th, a sub-committee was formed for the purpose of organising a deputation of women workers and their leaders, to bring before the notice of Queen Mary the stress and suffering of the paid women workers engendered by voluntary work.

This deputation, as a matter of fact, never presented itself at Buckingham Palace; for the simple reason that immediately Queen Mary was made aware of the state of affairs prevailing, she acted so promptly and effectively that the deputation was rendered unnecessary.

Her stroke was swift—and sure.

From many sides the news of the stress of the women workers had begun to be conveyed to Queen Mary, who was at once alive to its possibilities and dangers— and altogether in sympathy with the workers. She realised at the same time the need for voluntary work, and was of the conviction that, with organisation and intelligent handling, the voluntary work need not encroach on the domain of the workers.

Meanwhile her lady-in-waiting, also aware of the state of things, was besieging politicians and ministers to give the matter their attention.

"I appealed in vain," Lady Bertha Dawkins told me. "Everybody seemed too busy with something else, and in despair I at last went to the Queen, reporting my efforts and my failures.

"The Queen drew herself up angrily, and said: 'Well; they have got to attend to this matter.'

"And attend to it they did! How it all happened I do not know; but I do know that the Queen, personally, tapped various channels and promptly awoke ministerial interest, with the result that, in two days, action was taken. . . ."

Among the people who rendered invaluable help at this extremely difficult time was the Marchioness of Crewe, whom Queen Mary had summoned to Buckingham Palace. One of the first fruits of their cogitations was a letter, dated August 17th, 1914, from Queen Mary to the Workers' War Emergency Committee asking if that body "would be willing to suggest four or five women representatives of wage-earning women to advise and co-operate with a small sub-

country at large was prompt, overwhelming, and continuous.

But more of the Collecting Fund later.

The Central Committee, in its capacity both Advisory and Executive in this great effort, initiated by Queen Mary to keep trade where possible in the ordinary channels, to open up new trades for women, to start model workrooms in London to absorb women who were unemployed and, in connection with its central work, to advise mayoral and citizen committees which were being organised all over the country, how to conduct their work and to control them by grants from the Queen's Fund, represented Her Majesty's first contact with a definitely political organisation. Through the medium of the Central Committee, and in course of its working, it has already been pointed out, the Queen came personally in relation with leading Labour women (there was indeed a very strong contingent of them on the Committee); and throughout the whole war term of the Committee she was directly identified with the women workers and their welfare over the country.

It would seem hardly necessary to say, at this juncture, with what zest Queen Mary entered into the work of these organisations; how much of Mind she infused both into the creating and into the working of the various bodies.

The whole enterprise represented to her something new, something away from the beaten track of royal interests; something big, important, and human; something, dare one say, more worthy of her gifts and abilities. It was the least conventional of the war services she was called on to perform; it is part of her war work that is least known.

There is another aspect, too, I would emphasise; how eminently fitted she was to deal with this matter who as a girl of eighteen had been halted in her "coming out" by the Select Committee appointed by the House of Lords to enquire into the sweating system prevailing in the East End of London. Had not this adventure brought her most distressing experience in those years, and a sudden knowledge of the conditions of the women workers? Had she not burned with indignation at the state of women in the chain-making industry, for example, and with deadly purpose pursued every available means of finding out more, and at first hand, from Lord Dunraven, her mother's neighbour in Richmond, from books and pamphlets and the literature of industrial reform?

She had never forgotten the experience; she had never ceased to think of it. How often since then had she not gone incognito to the East End of London to see first hand how life was lived there: to *know*, and to know by no indirect and softened ways? The Bishop of London, speaking at Queen's College, Harley Street, in 1910, then confided to his audience how he, too, "had the pleasure" of showing Queen Mary privately something of the East side of London life.

"I can tell you," he said, "that there is no one who has more interest in all that makes for the welfare of the poor than our new Queen; no one who will bring such common sense and influence to bear on it; and no one who will do more for the general welfare of her people."

On the Central Committee, as a matter of fact, was one who could testify to the fact that, when the Sweated Industries Exhibition, organised at the Queen's Hall in May 1906, was nearing 'its end, Queen Mary, then Duchess of York, just returned from the endless fatigues of a tour in India, had immediately and in face of many protests that her immediate need was for rest, hastened to the Exhibition for fear of missing this opportunity again to learn about the industrial conditions of the women workers.

Miss Gertrude Tuckwell has recalled for me the thoroughness with which Her Royal Highness did find out things, and "surprised us by her knowledge of conditions, by her genuine sympathy and concern.

"I remember saying to one of her ladies in attendance during Her Royal Highness's tour of the Exhibition:

" 'Does it, I wonder, mean anything to her?'

" 'Mean anything!' came the emphatic reply. 'She will go straight home and read up every book available on what she has seen and heard. . . .' "

Here on the Central Committee was at least one woman who had figured in the Sweated Industries Exhibition at the Queen's Hall in 1906—Mary Macarthur; and other women there were who, more than most people Queen Mary met, could bring her up-to-date knowledge of the conditions of women workers from an angle that was peculiarly their own, and the workers', in a manner notably unvarnished, and, it must be said, new and refreshing to Queen Mary.

With characteristic cleverness, the Queen set out on the path of knowing. Here was no restraint—no

softening of the blow. The country was at war; the
Central Committee had been organised to serve the
country through the medium of relieving the distresses
of the women workers—distress which, as the Queen
well knew and saw, created a vital factor in the progress
of the War. If husbands and fathers and brothers were
busy fighting in the trenches, they were not altogether
oblivious or indifferent to the fate of the women they
had left behind, many of whom were receiving no War
Office allowances, but were left altogether dependent,
as usual, on what they earned by their labours.

Not a single detail of the working of the Central
Committee did Queen Mary allow to pass without her
knowledge. Her couriers were posted to fetch and
carry reports; her sage counsels were always at the
Committee's disposal. Although it was inevitable that
she held aloof, as it were, from the actual business of
the Committee yet was she as minutely informed of
all that happened, as if she had herself sat with the
Committee in Wimborne House, which had been lent by
Lady Wimborne for the first meetings.

The Central Committee grew and flourished and
strengthened with incredible speed. Her Majesty's
undivided support was always at its back: a potent
force which the Labour members of the Committee
were quick to realise, and not at all backward in putting
to use. Soon Wimborne House could no longer contain them, and Lady Clementine Waring kindly placed
at their disposal 8 and 9, Grosvenor Place, where the
administrative work was carried on; while various
branch offices of the Committee sprang up in all parts
of London for local work.

During the period of 1914-16 the Committee met thirty-one times. The sub-committees held numbered one hundred and eleven meetings. The first report of the work was published in 1915 at His Majesty's Stationery Office. It was presented to Parliament; and not without interest is the fact that it was the first report of a body of women ever presented at Westminster.

The work of the Central Committee in assisting the proper distribution of work available for women in ordinary industry and in providing alternative employment for skilled women workers displaced by the War was unremitting; and these two lines of activity largely occupied its earliest considerations. New avenues of permanent employment were pointed out and opened up; and the Committee also set down principles for the organisation of schemes of work for women unemployed, because of the War; considered and approved schemes submitted by local representatives for workrooms and training centres for women and girls over sixteen; opened up juvenile training centres and provided the materials for these centres.

Not the least intriguing aspect of the working of the Committee was the extreme and fundamentally divergent views of its various members. If these women were jointly effective in their fruits, and, to outward appearances, showed a united front, the inner courts were not without their "situations"—always interesting, often very amusing—sometimes instructive. But clashes and conflict of opinion among the members were among the elements to make the Committee the really live, spirited organisation that undoubtedly it was.

No one appreciated all this more than Queen Mary, who had, after all, brought it all about—had again related what it would have seemed impossible to relate; and had really welded together these diverse parts to an organic whole held the more firmly by her own inspiration, impregnated by her own personality.

The personal side of the Committee, if I may so distinguish, is extremely interesting in review and, by its various members I am assured, was no less interesting to those concerned at the time.

An incident which occurred at the first meeting of this extremely various body of women may perhaps best illustrate the unusualness, as it were, that everyone immediately began to discover in everyone else. It happened between the chairman, Lady Crewe, and the Hon. Secretary, Mary Macarthur, two women who had not met before, but "tremendously took to each other the very first time we met."

The result of that meeting, if I may digress for a moment, was a close and splendid friendship between Lady Crewe and Mary Macarthur. Miss Gertrude Tuckwell, one of the most intimate friends of Mary Macarthur, told me once: "Not long before Mary died she was reviewing to me her various friends and what each had meant to her in life. She came to Lady Crewe and of Lady Crewe she said, with rapt face: 'Ah! She has been such a precious and exquisite jewel in my life!'"

At this moment, however, the two women were meeting for the first time.

Introductions over, the ladies moved toward the Committee-rooms. On the threshold of the door Mary

Macarthur took occasion to whisper "rather terrify-
ingly" in the chairman's ear, as a last shot: "I, you
know, am a Tolstoyan!"

I do not know; but I feel that it would be safe to
assume that Lady Crewe smiled with perfect ease and
understanding, although at the time its effect was
"simply to appal me."

Thus, the chairman struggling with her forebodings,
and wondering "what on earth it meant to be a Tolstoyan, and if it was quite as bad as it sounded," the
first sitting of the Central Committee began.

This was but a mild stirring compared with the much
in store, not alone for the chairman; for the Committee had its markedly disputatious minds, and all the
members were more or less spirited women.   There
were times when high Tory notions came violently
athwart the pacifism of one of the most unpacific and
pugnacious Labour members; and there were those not
necessarily of Tory persuasion who "invariably chose
the most critical moment to air some stupidity relating
to a particular industrial trouble of the moment."   (I
borrow the description from a detached observer.)

I am tempted to linger on the "delightful insolence"
as Dr. Marion Philips once described it to me, of the
chairman when she was dealing with these stupidities
and her "extraordinary effectiveness" therein; but I
must content myself by repeating what again a more or
less neutral observer (politically) remarked to me as
she reflected on the time:

"It was not that the Labour women were incapable
of defending themselves or their party.   On the contrary; only nothing they ever did or said ever had

that deadly bite and incisiveness of the chairman's occasional most charmingly delivered remarks at these trying times."

"Looking back at the names of the Committee members," said Miss Gertrude Tuckwell, "representing Conservatives, Liberal, Die-hard, and Labour, one feels that such unanimity would have been impossible had it not been that a great emergency rouses that patriotism which is above party, and that all were united in the work of salvage."

Queen Mary at Buckingham Palace, posted in every detail of the working of the Committee, was also aware and very appreciative of the different personalities who composed the Committee. She wasted no opportunity that, by direct or indirect means, might bring her closer to understanding of the point of view of the Labour members.

And here a tremendously interesting thing happened. There came a meeting between the royal patron of the Committee and its honorary secretary, Mary Macarthur, the "Tolstoyan" and Women's Trade Union organiser, "when," as Miss Tuckwell has remarked, "Mary did first pioneer the Labour party to the presence of monarchy."

Mary Macarthur's views on the institution of royalty, familiar enough to all who knew her, were notably unchanged by recent happenings; but she was a woman of sense, as well as of considerable experience of the world, and was not unaware of the value and significance of the Central Committee to the interests of the workers. Also she was aware of the value of Queen

Mary's support and patronage and its influence on the country as a whole.

All this she had wit to realise long before her meeting with Queen Mary—a meeting which, as is known, brought to Mary Macarthur, "the slip of a girl from Ayr," when first she came to London with a purpose no more and no less than to free the women workers from the bondage of the sweating system and organise them into Trades Unions—many new and strange experiences.

These experiences were not uncostly to Mary Macarthur, but how little she was fundamentally changed by them is delightfully shown in a story that is told of a visit to the country home of one of her "new friends." In the afternoon, it seems, "Mary took one of the other women guests for a long walk in the country," and on the way back remarked casually, waving her hand at the stately pile: "These manorial homes, you know, will all one day be museums for the people!"

What the lady said is not recorded.

In truth, to Mary Macarthur as to other members of the Central Committee, these "new friends" were at first "something of a joke." The association continued to be a joke until, in the course of time and events, Mary Macarthur came personally and directly in contact with Queen Mary: an incident which forms the first chapter of an extraordinarily romantic if unknown story, called by certain women members of the Labour Party "the Case of Mary Am and Mary R," Miss Helena Normanton has told me.

It was the meeting of two women. When Mary Macarthur at length recovered from the shock of meet-

ing a great woman upon obediently presenting herself
at Buckingham Palace in response to the summoning of
a Queen, she was quite overwhelmed by the discovery
of the woman that was Queen Mary.

To the lasting credit of Mary Macarthur it must be
said that, having the sense and the vision at once to
perceive the manner of woman she had met at Buckingham Palace, she had also the courage—and it needed
courage—not to conceal the discovery from her "comrades" in the Movement. Indeed, far from resting in
the merely negative attitude of not concealing her discovery, she told it to all whom she met. Right and
left she broadcast the news.

What this courage and this honesty has cost Mary
Macarthur in the good opinion of sections of the Movement, is apparent now that she is dead. It is, however,
comforting to remember that in life she was much too
big to bother about such trivial criticisms and dis-
approvals.

In certain quarters her whole association with the
Queen was suspect; and Mary went blithely on, positively revelling in this new experience and, with her
customary shrewd Scottish sense, never letting an opportunity slip. "Mary," said Miss Tuckwell, "was
always and essentially businesslike, of a habit of seizing
hold on every available means and purpose to further
the Cause she was espousing."

One hopes, and one has reason to believe, that neither
Her Majesty nor Mary Macarthur were oblivious to
or unappreciative of the strangely different courses of
their lives and their experiences; that, added to all else,

there was for both an element of romance in the meeting.

Place—power—rank—social differences as such never did have, never could have had, less effect on these two women who met in the setting of Buckingham Palace, compared with the mutual recognition which came to each of sincerity, strength, genuineness, and character, and the longing to help which, after all, was the motivating force in each and which had been responsible for their meeting.

Vastly different as were their personalities, totally and fundamentally divergent as were their experiences of life, they yet discovered a singular sameness in their attitude to life which rendered differences of character, differences in experience alike to infinite unimportance.

Instinctively they seized hold of this sameness, and on it was based their whole relationship, their mutual respect and regard.

Mary Macarthur, like the essentially big woman she was, left her trifling comrades to rattle the bones, and build their hypotheses from out of the vapours of their distorted imaginations. Her own attitude is well summed up in her shout of delight to Miss Tuckwell when she came back from her first meeting with the Queen.

"Here is someone who *can* and who *means* to help!"

The mutual respect and regard, engendered at the first meeting of these two women, strengthened and deepened as time passed. It is a matter of fact that the sudden and lamentable death of Mary Macarthur came as a personal loss to Queen Mary of England; and two of the last things that this noble-hearted woman said and did the day before her death, related to her "new friend." She pencilled a note to Lady Roxburgh referring to the Queen the night before she died, "and which did not come to me until she was dead," Lady Roxburgh has told me.

"I remember so well that day," said Miss Tuckwell, relating the second of these circumstances to me, "as I came into the bedroom, Mary raised herself on the bed and said with a flicker of a smile of pleasure in her face: 'H.M. sent me a message this morning!'"

She sank back in the bed, and died soon after.

Queen Mary's great sympathy and understanding—her intelligence, so free from the limitations that would seem more than pardonable in a queen—her values in human relationship—it is these qualities that again stand out in her friendship with Mary Macarthur. The humility of Queen Mary; her deep, unfeigned desire to know and to understand matters remote from her life, expressing itself in such ways as a request to Mary Macarthur for lists of books she might read on whatever subject was under discussion at the time—it was such things as these that touched Mary Macarthur to the core. Here was someone who really cared! It was all that mattered.

One does not marvel that:

"Mary's appreciation and administration of the Queen grew unbounded," as I have been told by one who worked closely with her at this time.

" 'Always,' Mary would say, 'Her Majesty was so kind, so courteous, so genuine. The point is,' she would reiterate, 'the Queen simply does understand and grasp the whole situation from the Trades Union point of view. She does understand.' "

To Mary Macarthur, as to many another, this understanding was always somehow too good almost to be true.

From the Queen, Mary Macarthur also took strength —inspiration, as had so many people before her. At frequent intervals during her visits to Buckingham Palace or when Queen Mary visited her at home, in Mecklenburgh Square, she improved the shining hours, presenting the Trades Union point of view in her exuberant, incorrigible way.

Or again it was: "To-day I positively lectured the Queen on the inequality of the classes—the injustice of things. . . . I fear that I talked too much again."

It was a simple, human relationship. "Well, Mary," she was asked on her return from her first meeting with the Queen, "and did you back out from Her Majesty's presence?"

"No," said Mary firmly; "not being a gymnast, I did not."

Most delightful was "Mary's endeavour to behave herself in the presence of the Queen," and the "dreadful confusion" that overtook her from time to time from very trying.

"You see," she would explain ruefully, "it never occurred to me that when the Queen rose it was my signal to go."

Says Miss Tuckwell, "Invariably she would conclude her story: 'But there, of course, the Queen will understand!' "

.   .   .   .   .   .

In spite of the hectic clash of personalities, the stupidities of some and the stupendous revelations that came to others, the Central Committee flourished, "helped out no little," as all agree, by Lady Crewe's "breadth of outlook" and Mrs. Tennant's "Labour sympathies." Behind the Committee always was the power of the Queen, who, with her intimate knowledge of women in industry, a knowledge enlarged and brought up to date by frequent sessions with Mary Macarthur, put her whole mind into the schemes and plans projected by the Committee. Also the Committee was well supported by an expert board of commercial and official advisers, who worked with the Government Committee and local committees. Mr. J. J. Mallon, secretary of the Anti-Sweating League, was from the beginning prominently associated with the Committee. "His help," Lady Roxburgh has told me, "was invaluable. When things went wrong, or seemed threatening, the cry was always, 'Oh, do see Mr. Mallon!'"

"Not charity, but work!" In the very watch-word of the Committee was the ring of its royal patron and inspirer. Hers was a high purpose, and Miss Margaret Bondfield has said of the achievement: "What Queen Mary did through the Central Committee was to save the self-respect of countless women workers."

Economically, as Queen Mary well knew, the isolated woman worker was the weakest in the community.

"We are, or ought to be," she said on one occasion, "now more than ever members of one body; and one of our first tasks is to help this, the weakest and least organised section of the working class, to 'carry on.'

Given the means and the machinery, it ought not to be impossible to find work for women to do. . . ."

It was not found impossible. In course of time and by virtue of its great growth, the Central Committee's activities were allocated to Sub-committees and, as these began to function, they did excellent work. Workrooms were opened everywhere to demonstrate to local Representative Committees how to relieve distress in their own immediate neighbourhoods without dislocating trade. The attention of the Committee was drawn to the conditions in the manufacture of hosiery, and Queen Mary immediately placed an order with the Committee for the purchase of woolen belts to form part of "The Queen's gift to the Troops," which enabled the Committee to order wool from spinners whose staffs were only partially occupied. The actual making of the belts was given to other firms with unemployed women on their hands. It is interesting to note that the yarn for the making of these seventy-five thousand belts was ordered from firms previously engaged in producing yarn for carpets, a commodity for which, with war in progress, there was now little call.

I do not intend to cite categorically individual firms and specific sections of industry which, in many cases, owed their very existence to the orders which issued from the Central Committee; or which were restrained from closing their shops by a timely order. It is, however, of interest to note as typical the case of a London dressmaker whose business, usually employing more than a hundred women, was brought to an absolute standstill very early in the War.

On learning of Her Majesty's schemes for the em-

ployment of women, the head of the firm asked leave
to tender for a number of the belts which were to form
part of the gift of Queen Mary to the troops. Her
tender was accepted, and she was congratulated for her
celerity in seizing upon this chance. She proceeded to
purchase the required wool and machinery, and set
about training her staff to the new occupation. The
first contract entrusted to her, and amounting to fifteen
hundred pounds, being completed promptly and to the
satisfaction of the Committee, the Committee put her
in line for permanent army contracts in hosiery, on
which her workers continued to be fully employed.

Like mushrooms in the night local workrooms sprang
up everywhere in London and outside of London. In
some they made cradles from banana-crates; in others
maternity outfits and appurtenances for the sickroom.
New clothes were made from old; fruit was preserved,
and in the training centres, women were trained in
market gardening, fruit and flower growing, as well
as for all ramifications of domestic science. This all in
the early days of the Committee, and over and above
their contracting, which already had brought them into
relations with more than a hundred firms whose workers
had been thrown out of employment by the War.

All the ingenuity that the brain of women could devise was applied to the purpose of giving work rather
than charity to the women of England. To the organisation of the Committee the Queen gave punctilious care and attention. No appointment, great or
small, was made without her knowledge; not a report
was issued without her full awareness.

Her interest took on from time to time an even more

intimate and practical turn. Afternoons were spent at
the various workrooms, and her visits were anything
but perfunctory. She toured the offices; she toured
the workrooms; up and down stairs she went, and
poked in every corner. She held long and extremely
edifying discussions with the various chief accountants,
examining books and return-sheets from the various
individual workrooms. Heads of departments were
presented to her; and with the heads of departments
she discussed the conditions and progress of the departments themselves. She examined samples submitted to the Committee; samples of wool, flannel, and
suchlike materials. . . .

Nothing escaped her; and she was in her element.

The experiences which resulted from these tours were
not, however, all for Queen Mary. For the first time,
many Labour women saw some fraction of the formalities which hedge about a Queen. Always there were
presentations to be made of the various officials, of the
various heads of departments, usually conducted by the
chairman or secretary of the Committee. Invariably
there was a battery of cameras to be faced, a crowd to
be managed. How with such endless fallalery, how
with such interminable hand-shaking, it was possible
for a human being to find the requisite detachment, not
to say time, for intelligent interest in the workrooms
was something that passed the understanding of the
"Labour" women looking on.

As they watched the regal figure so courteously and
graciously disposing of this phalanx of formality, their
admiration increased by leaps and bounds. . . .

Mary Macarthur, in her office of the Central Com-

mittee in Wimborne House, and later at 8 Grosvenor
Place, "a ballroom illumined only by artificial light,"
received the royal patron at intervals, and eagerly
poured out the latest happenings. The visit she had
made to *The Times*, for example, because she felt that
it was not giving the amount of space appropriate to
the Committee's work; how she had gone to obtain an
interview with Lord Northcliffe; of her impressions
of Lord Northcliffe; of her inspection with him of the
offices in Printing House Square; of her success with
him—for Lord Northcliffe had promptly given instructions that the Committee should be given publicity
in *The Times*. It is known how, later, the work of
the Central Committee was given due recognition and
considerable space in *The Times' History of the War*.

I cannot exaggerate the sheer inspiration which these
women found in the presence of the Queen, with her
calm, capacious, orderly mind, her genuine interest and
concern.

Again and again, to officials small and great of the
various Funds, Committees united in this great effort
to provide "Work, not Charity," to the thousands of
working women threatened by destitution soon after
the outbreak of war, she would reiterate:

"Even if it does seem a detail, it matters to me.
Let me know everything!"

And so far as it was possible, she did know everything—from the sending of an ambulance to France,
says Lady Roxburgh, to the details of the wrapping of
socks sent to the trenches. To all of this she brought
the same intense concern, and, as much as anything, it
explains her success. With a thoroughness that was

disconcerting, she applied her businesslike mind to the scrutiny of finances and reports: and invariably said quite frankly what she thought.

An offer of specially favourable terms of emigration having been made to the Queen on behalf of certain Australian governments, representatives were appointed by the Committee to act as a special emigration Committee under the chairmanship of Mrs. Lewis, now Viscountess Harcourt.

During one of the busiest mornings of the War, amidst the multitude of letters that surrounded her, came a letter to Queen Mary from a woman emigrant sent to Australia with the help of the Central Committee. The latter noted one or two circumstances which had attended the landing, and which, the writer felt, might well be different.

Lady Harcourt was promptly summoned: "I beg of you to see to this matter of the landing," said Her Majesty. "It does seem to me most important that these things should not happen at the landing. . . ."

When it was found necessary to form many sub-committees of the Central Committee as the Fund swelled and unemployment increased, and the variegated nature of the undertaking came home to the members of the Central Committee, Her Majesty was conferred with on matters of appointment no less than on matters of procedure.

In the securing and placing of contracts her guidance and advice was invaluable to the Central Committee, and, "as if she had been accustomed to the handling of Big Business all her life," when the Royal Army Clothing Department surrendered to the Committee the whole business of the cutting and making of army shirts, it was Queen Mary's mind also that planned the where and when of setting up special "cutting" workshops, engaging a whole staff of cutters under the supervision of the general secretary of the Shirt and Jacket Cutters' Union, foreman of the new venture.

Meanwhile, the Collecting Fund and its powerful Committee and Lady Roxburgh's inexhaustible enthusiasm canvassed up and down the country with their spirited appeals drafted by Queen Mary.

"Surely," wrote the Queen, in one manifesto, "the appeal will not be in vain to women with comfortable homes and sufficient means to keep their own families from the pinch of want. . . ."

The response was eminently worthy. Money came from every section of the public, from pennies to hundreds of pounds. The subscriptions averaged £1,000 a day; £20,000 was subscribed in the first twelve hours of the fund's existence.

These sums were not too much for the providing of work to the 45,000 women in London alone who on September 5th, 1914, formed the melancholy procession that besieged the offices of the Queen's Central Committee at Wimborne House.

During 1915 the demand for women's labour increased so largely, owing to the requirements of the Services and the needs of the War Industries, that there was little industrial distress in the ranks of women workers except among small sections of the community, which continued in the care of the Central Committee.

XVI

OTHER duties, other organisations were pressing for the help of the Queen, and, with a like completeness of service, she turned her attention to the new needs.

In the space of one year, the first year of the War, in the midst of a thousand and one claims on her time and support, Her Majesty had, with the loyal support of those splendid women who composed the Central Committee, the help of the women of the whole Empire who provided the funds, relieved King George and his Government from the threatened peril of industrial trouble so that they might the better concentrate on the conduct of the War.

It was a magnificent piece of work, about which all too little is known, and, while the Central Committee still goes on under a Government department, the closing scenes of its war-time phase were movingly enacted at the Mary Macarthur Memorial Home, Ongar, July 28th, 1924, when the presence of Her Majesty, the Queen, the Marchioness of Crewe, Mrs. H. J. Tennant, Dr. Marion Philips, and other members of the Central Committee come to pay tribute to the woman to whose memory, and in whose honour, they had erected the Home as a place in which, from time to time, those women workers, in whose behalf

Mary Macarthur had devoted her life, might rest from their labours.

No one that was present at Ongar will easily forget the scene with Queen Mary, dressed in pale mauve, with her bouquet of pink and mauve malmaisons grown in Mrs. Tennant's gardens at Maytham, and presented by Nancy Anderson, the only child of Mary Macarthur; women of the Labour Party; women of the Court, with the company leavened by a party of working girls taking their holiday at the Home—a cigarmaker from Houndsditch, an old office-cleaner, a girl clerk, a laundry "hand," and so on.

There were one or two short speeches. Queen Mary was reminded, in a brief address delivered by a friend of Mary Macarthur's, how that "Until the end she [Mary Macarthur] experienced your gracious friendship and deeply valued it. You, by your presence to-day, have shown that the three years which have elapsed since her death have not blurred her memory. . . ."

Her Majesty, with an economy of words, not easily delivered, then paid tribute to the memory of Mary Macarthur; and there was not a woman in the strange medley of women there foregathered, who was not stirred to the depths by the absolute simplicity and sincerity of those few unstudied words.

XVII

WITH her horror of waste, her intolerance of activity without intelligent purpose, it may be imagined with what resolution Queen Mary turned to the Needlework Guild that already bore her name, by means of which she aspired to direct the epidemic of knitting and sewing that afflicted women throughout the Empire immediately on outbreak of war.

The spirit was willing, the intention good; and no one can easily forget the melancholy sight of women in trains, tubes, restaurants, concerts, public meetings, doing something with their fingers as though their very lives depended on it; as if the loss of a moment, much less a stitch, meant tragedy for the nation.

The results of this movement were altogether abnormal; much of the production was valueless from the point of view of the men of the Service for whom it was destined; and none too early Queen Mary stepped in, more or less to save the situation.

For many years there had been in existence a Needlework Guild. Queen Mary inherited it, with much other of her mother's Titanic charity legacy. It had originally been inspired by the late Lady Wolverton, a near neighbour to the Duchess of Teck at Richmond, and one of Her Royal Highness's great friends. (It was with Lady Wolverton that Princess May and her mother went abroad after the death of the Duke of Clarence.)

Mr. Galsworthy has said that "to sew and knit and do useful things with their fingers is bred into women." Lady Wolverton's ambition seems to have been to resolve the immense amount of needlework thrown off by most women in the course of the year into one big effort for systematic distribution to the poor. The "power of the united Littles," she called it.

Lady Wolverton took her scheme to the Queen's mother, Princess Mary Adelaide, who, need one say, boisterously seized hold on the idea, and so thoroughly did she electrify it that soon there was hardly a county in the Kingdom without its branch of the Needlework Guild. In 1910 there were one hundred centres of the Guild in England and Wales alone; and the garments contributed alone by Queen Mary in 1910 numbered no less than 15,333, including mits and cuffs made by her children, which, "I am afraid," she remarked on the occasion, "cost some tears; for stitches had to be picked up and mistakes made good. . . ."

In those early days the "comforters," contributed by "Bertie" (the Duke of York), usually arrived without a label; while "David" was conspicuously careful always to mark his handiwork, comforters like his brother "Bertie's," made on a frame.

One of the large galleries of the Imperial Institute, Kensington, was used for the yearly distribution of the Guild's prolific fruits; and annually the Queen, head of the Guild, arrived with apron, scissors, and much other businesslike equipment to help wrap up socks, unpack parcels, and repack for ultimate distribution.

When the crisis came the Queen summoned to Buckingham Palace a small Committee to take hold of the existing machinery of the Guild, of which Her Majesty was President; and the council was formed on which Queen Mary sat simply as a member, to direct the voluntary needlework of the women of the Empire.

The Committee included Princess Mary, Lady Savory, Mrs. Harcourt, the Hon. Mrs. Mallet, Miss Farquhar, Lady Lawley, Lady Northcliffe, Lady Dawson, Lady Ampthill, Lady Bertha Dawkins, Miss Halford, Miss Taylor-Whitehead, and Miss Allcroft.

It was an eminently respectable body, doing work thoroughly approved by those among others who might have felt uneasy about the Central Committee, and spoke their thought loudly about the Marchioness of Londonderry and her uniformed "Legion," in the pioneer days of the formation of that body.

On August 10th the first council was held. King George lent the Levee suite of rooms at Friary Court, St. James's Palace, for the Guild.

Soon, throughout the world, Friary Court was known as the great clearing-house for voluntary gifts. In ten months 1,101,105 articles were received, ranging from beautiful old embroidered towels, family heirlooms sent by Russian peasants—to the handiwork of native Zulu chiefs; and St. James's Palace became more like a dry-goods store every day, with the room in which Charles I spent his last night filled with enough pairs of pyjamas to have served his successors to this day.

Every State in the United States of America sent its offerings to the Queen; the Dominions, as ever, sent generously and in overwhelming profusion; from

neutral countries, including those of South America,
came regular contributions.   Canada had its branches
of the Guild, and the United States.

This was all magnificent.   It thrilled the Queen.
The supply did not exceed the need; but what sheer
business ability and ingenuity it required to prevent
over-lapping or encroachment on the industrial territory of working women may safely be left to the
imagination.

In this matter Lady Lawley was supreme, for her
great gifts of organisation; and she was indefatigable.

Gradually every room in St. James's Palace began
to be filled with clothing, except the Throne Room,
whose doors were shut on this new, incongruous reality.
The very heart of the Guild's activities throughout the
War was in the Tapestry Room of the Palace, whence
the workers looked down on the Colour Court built by
Henry VIII.   The secretarial work was carried on in
Queen Anne's Drawing-room next door; the Armoury
Room, which completed the historic suite, where the
very walls seemed to tell of the Kings and Queens who
lived there in the past, was also now in use by the
Guild.

The packers occupied Colour Court, and, whether
gifts came from the Shetlands, Truro, Putney, Montreal, or Dunedin, they were piled in the Colour Court
built by Henry VIII.

"To the Queen" the parcels came in a steady stream
from over the seas, their contents to be first "entered"
in Queen Anne's Drawing-rooms—rooms which to-
day stand unaltered since the time when Charles II
trifled with bowls with the ladies of his Court or in the

stiff, unchildish dress of the times, played games with his brother and sister.

After being recorded the contents went down the wide corridor where the children of Charles I chattered and played, out into the Colour Court, to be packed into a fourgon from the royal mews standing on the paving-stones which were laid under the very eyes of Henry VIII—to be sent away again "From the Queen" to the fighting men.

From the first day of the Guild's efforts, when two or three handkerchiefs and shirts straggled in, up to the very end, when some fifteen and a half million of things had been distributed from Friary Court, one aim had been set before the management, emanating from the Queen: Provide what is wanted, where it is wanted, in the shortest possible time. And: Away with Red Tape!

With the rout of Red Tape, there set in a wonderful time for those who tended the sick and wounded and men in Service. Any hospital or commanding office could get what they wanted, from a single splint to 20,-000 surgical requisites; from a shirt to 6,000 pairs of socks—all despatched within twenty-four hours of the request.

By November 1918 there were 630 branches of Queen Mary's Needlework Guild and a membership of 1,078,839, not including the branches in the United States and Canada.

On hospital clothing and the accessories of healing the Guild specialised, and in other comforts for the wounded men; and clothing went to necessitous families in one long uninterrupted flow in the early days before

industry recovered from the impact of the first months
of war.

To Belgian refugees, to our prisoners of war, went
out yet more succour and warmth through this great
organisation, and literally millions sterling were saved
from the coffers of the nation by the voluntary labour
in the surgical supply depots, and their equipment also
organised in the Guild.

The benevolences of Queen Mary's Needlework
Guild encircled the entire war-sick, ravaged world—
from the Allied Forces in France to the forces in South
Africa, in East Africa and Egypt. To 744 regiments
it distributed; to 304 hospitals at home and 216 hos-
pitals abroad, including Serbia and the Dardanelles;
to Camps and Convalescent homes throughout the
"Allied" world. It assisted 207 Soldiers' and Sailors'
Families Association Committees; the Officers' Families
Fund, the India Fund, and the Royal Navy.

Again Her Majesty, Queen Mary, was the guiding
star, the sustained inspiration.

How many shirts went on the backs of the men in
France—not until they had passed through her hands,
satisfied her examination—she from whom a high standard of shirts had been exacted many years in her
own household.

And when shirts and socks were to go to the Dardanelles, it was Queen Mary who, on examination, and
with intimate knowledge of climate, decided that they
were too thick for wear in such hot weather.

In the first twenty-six months, 3,990,784 garments
went out from the Guild, and, as winter came round

again, a second appeal went out from the Queen for winter comforts for the troops:

"The response to my first appeal has exceeded all expectations; but we have not yet arrived at the moment for any relaxation of our efforts in this direction, especially as the winter is approaching. I appeal once more to the loyalty and love shown me by the women of the Empire, with confidence that they will continue in the future the splendid and generous support which I have been accorded in the past. . . ."

XVIII

APART from over and above the vast organisation of women who looked to Queen Mary for direct initiative, enthusiasm and continued inspiration—the Needlework Guild stretching octopus-like from Kensington to Tokyo, the ramifications of the nursing profession and the amazing V.A.D.'s, to mention only two colossal organisations of the woman power of the Empire—her "surplus" energies were called on in a hundred and one directions. Wherever she turned, to whatsoever she set her hand, there some desolated woman was to be comforted for the loss of a son, a husband; and almost every day the ravages of war were vividly to be seen in a hospital whose wards were filled with troops fresh from the battlefields.

It is well-nigh appalling to realise the number of the various tragedies and enterprises into which Queen Mary was drawn during the course of the war. Hers was no formal interest; she gave of her own self; and the ideas she conceived, the schemes and plans she originated, show, on examination, in all directions.

Always there were hostels to visit as well as hospitals; to nurseries and crêches she went; war shrines; munition factories; workshops where in green glass goggles she watched the training of new workers in oxy-acetylene welding. There were troops to be visited with the King; and while His Majesty was recovering from

his accident in the field, Queen Mary herself inspected
the troops on behalf of the King.   Two of her own sons
were at the war; and there was no end to the casual-
ties constantly reported of her various household
staffs. . . .

Miss Lilian Barker, the vigilant mother of the pro-
digious army of women munition workers at Woolwich,
who is now making new history in His Majesty's peni-
tentiary for women and girls at Borstal, has given me
a moving account of the Queen's association with those
countless women munition workers.

"I never saw such wild enthusiasm among those
thousands of women as when Her Majesty came to
see them one day," Miss Barker told me. "They simply
worshipped her, and watched with unbelieving eyes as
she went here and there, in and out—wherever she
chose to go.

"Then, she announced her wish to go into the danger
buildings—a wish we had not anticipated, a happening
for which we were not prepared.   There was, however,
no gainsaying her; and so into the danger huts she
went, armoured as the women who worked there were
armoured, in a respirator, goloshes, taking the same
risks as the next woman; for the dangers were so great,
the explosives so high-powered, that the women had
to work in separate little huts for fear of explosion, and
in order to minimise the loss of life in such an event.

"There was nothing she missed in the whole of the
Woolwich area given over to the women munition
workers.   In every canteen and kitchen she went, ply-
ing us with questions as to how the girls were fed;
how they were protected; what arrangements we had

for accident emergencies—she was so untiring, so absolutely sincere. . . ." And Miss Barker, every now and then, and with her characteristic vehemence and finality, would break off the thread of her glowing narrative with: "Sincere? Well; I've met a few women in my time, but from my heart, I never knew a more sincere woman than Queen Mary. This is what the girls felt."

There came work abroad for Her Majesty to perform, work in France: a brief, hectic term of service—ten days, to be precise—into which was pressed ten months of harrowing experience that was not, however, without its thrill of adventure for the Queen, who set out with perhaps more than her usual keenness. The official object of the visit was largely for the benefit of the nurses on active service, and, while this end was fulfilled, much additional work was actually achieved.

The visit was planned and arranged in great secrecy; and only after repeated representations had been made to the King, pointing out and emphasising how greatly Her Majesty's presence in France would be appreciated by the nurses, the men sick in hospitals, the many women engaged in other various forms of service, the motor-drivers and ambulance women, and the cooks of the Women's Legion.

So it came about that on July 3rd, 1917, Her Majesty left Victoria Station at 8.30 for France, with Lady Airlie, who was to be her sole companion on the projected errand of mercy. Not more than three or four people in London were aware of the royal mission; and Lady Airlie tells us, not without pride, that "even though my son was to be married in a few days, I did

not even tell him: a fact he found hard to forgive!"

King George accompanied the Queen and Lady
Airlie to Calais, where, after lunching inadequately at
the station—and incidentally having "our first experience of the impossibility of getting food," as Lady Airlie described it—His Majesty took leave of the Queen,
who proceeded alone to her chateau at Montreuil,
which, for the time being, served them as headquarters,
and whence the two ladies started with the dawn each
morning on their protracted daily tours.

From early morning until late at night, with little
intermission, Her Majesty worked tirelessly. The field
of her mission covered a wide area, and life in France,
at least for the Queen, seemed to present what Lady
Airlie has called one long, unending vista of hospitals.

From hospital to hostel Queen Mary progressed;
and again from hostel to hospital—driving long dis-
tances in the sweltering heat of those July days, living
precariously, and being heartily grateful if there was
a cup of coffee to be had mid-morning—for the travellers set forth so early—returning again to her château
in Montreuil at night to recover as best she could from
the physical and emotional stress of the day, and prepare for the next morning and its long, unending vista
of hospitals.

Lady Airlie has told me: "However many hospitals
Her Majesty visited a day, she spoke to every single
patient in them. Not a solitary one did she miss."
Generals commanding, no less than Medical Directors,
matrons, nurses, and the men in bed could only "wonder how on earth it was humanly possible for a woman

to sustain from day to day what Her Majesty was called on to sustain, to go through what she did go through," yet always to be ready for the next call on her sympathy, her consolation, her compassion, her practical help and advice.

In the suffocating heat, over long and dirty roads, the army car hummed with its gracious occupant. Nothing was left to chance, to accident; so far as things could be planned beforehand, the Queen saw to it that they were planned: time was short; and there was a superhuman task to be got through.

"Please do not follow too close behind me in the wards," the Queen said one day to Lady Airlie. "You see, I can talk more easily to the men if I am alone." Alone she made her circuits of the wards, speaking individually to each man; while those who watched were "simply stunned"—and it was all so personal, so moving a sight.

Yet other experiences, other sights came from time to time to interrupt the long vista of hospitals. There was a day at Audriques, when Her Majesty and Lady Airlie were taken to a camouflage factory to see the gun-screens made to look like growths of trees. They saw, too, the preparation of liquid fire.

"Until that moment," said Lady Airlie, with an involuntary shudder of horror at the memory, "I do not think one had quite realised what war meant."

They went over the despoiled battlefields, where they saw bits of children's toys, photographs, remnants of clothing, and other distressing evidences of an army pursuing and a civilian population in flight; and Lady Airlie vividly summed up for me the memory of those days in a picture she drew of an "old, old farm-woman" they met one day, hoeing potatoes on her farm. As she hoed, the old woman would stop now and then, put her head one side, and mumble, as she looked away in the distance:

"Always the sound of those guns. Day and night; always the sound of those guns."

And she would again turn to hoe her potatoes, while far away the dull, steady chorus of the guns continued. . . .

.   .   .   .   .   .

It was, of course, altogether what one would predict of Queen Mary that, when the vilifications of the W.A.A.C.'s were as lurid as they could be, and as spiteful, the slanderous assaults on their moral conduct not to be excelled in ludicrous calumny, she should permit herself to be appointed Commandant-in-Chief of the organisation to "mark her appreciation" of its "splendid service."

The announcement of the appointment of Queen Mary as Commandant-in-Chief of the much-maligned W.A.A.C.'s synchronised with the first public bestowal of a bouquet on the Corps in the form of an official pronouncement by the Army Council, April 20th, 1918, telling of the bravery of the Corps during the "big push" of April 1918.

"One party of W.A.A.C.'s employed at an Army School within the area of operations were offered transport to convey them to a safer locality farther back," ran the announcement. "They, however, refused to avail themselves of it on the ground that it would probably be wanted for something more important, and they marched fifteen miles back to the place to which they had been ordered. After all the students at the school had gone, they remained there in a dangerous position feeding relays of tired and hungry officers and men, and assisting in every way possible before they were compelled to leave the place.

"All reports, the War Office states, bear out the fact that the W.A.A.C.'s during the crisis have more than justified their existence and have well maintained the credit of their sex and of the Army to which they belong."

Lord Derby, Secretary of State, was always one of the most enthusiastic supporters of the Women's Corps; and it has always been assumed by those at the head of the Corps that Lord Derby's gallant espousal of the organisation and his representations to Queen Mary had much to do with Her Majesty's ultimate assumption of leadership at a time when she was already loaded with burdens that might well have wearied a super-woman.

There was a rather pathetic suggestion of this in the new Commandant-in-Chief's meeting with Dame Florence Leach, Controller-in-Chief, when she was summoned to Windsor. "I am afraid," said the Queen, "I cannot do much actual work; but I will do everything in my power."

I have been assured by Dame Leach that "above all else, Her Majesty helped us to live down the slanders of the past." To her Controller-in-Chief the Commandant gave "renewed courage, immeasurable impetus; a more than reward for anything that had happened in the past. . . . Her Majesty became," continued Dame Leach, "our strongest support; our inspiration."

"A thrill of inestimable pride ran through the whole Corps! In their keeping was the name of Queen Mary, Commandant-in-Chief. . . ."

There was a story, and I have since confirmed it with Dame Leach, which excellently shows the sustained and far-reaching effects on the moral and standard of the W.A.A.C.'s of their new leadership. One need not emphasise, surely, that the story reflects on the gallantry and "forthrightness" of the section of the American Expeditionary Force, whom also the story concerned.

It related to a battalion of one thousand W.A.A.C.'s "loaned to us," according to Colonel David L. Stone, of the General Staff Command, with the A.E.F., "through the courtesy of the British War Office, a battalion composed of young women of the British Empire."

"I spoke to each girl before she left for France to join the A.E.F.," Dame Leach told me. "I looked each one straight in the eyes. . . . I reminded them of their Commandant-in-Chief; and that also they would represent to the American Army the women of the whole British Empire."

During the whole of their ensuing service with the American Army there was not, among those thousand girls, a single case of misconduct—moral, or of any other description.

Courtesies were exchanged between the Colonel of the General Staff commanding at the Headquarters of the United States Troops, Bourges (Cher) France, and the Headquarters of the Queen Mary's Army Auxiliary Corps, Grosvenor Street, London, on June 27th, 1919.

"With genuine regret," wrote Colonel Stone, "the receipt of orders relieving the Q.M.A.A.C. battalion from duty at the Central Records Office is announced. This battalion, composed of young women of the British Empire, was loaned to us through the courtesy of the British War Office, and its members have been of invaluable help in preparing and maintaining an accurate record of our forces in the A.E.F.

"The conduct of these young women under surroundings absolutely new to them, working in daily association with men from another army, and whom they had never seen before, has been such as to gain for them the admiration and commendation of all persons, both civil and military, in this community. They have entered with interest and enthusiasm into all our athletic sports, entertainments, etc., and have proven themselves to be thorough sportswomen and have contributed in large part to the success of all events in which they entered.

"On behalf of all members of this command, I wish to say *au revoir* and God-speed to these young ladies, who have proven themselves to be a credit to their officers, to their chief who organised and commands their corps, and to their country."

From Dame Leach, Controller-in-chief, came the reply for Queen Mary's Army Auxiliary Corps:

"May I ask you, on behalf of myself and all officials and members of Queen Mary's Auxiliary Corps, who

AUTOGRAPHED PHOTOGRAPH OF QUEEN MARY, WITH HER
FIRST GRANDCHILD, "LITTLE GEORGIE LASCELLES"

have had the honour of working with the American
Expeditionary Force in Bourges, Tours, and Paris, to
express to all officers and other ranks our most grateful
thanks for the wonderful way in which they received
and accepted the service of the Corps.

"Had it not been for the splendid spirit of good-
fellowship and co-operation which was shown to us in
the beginning and throughout our service with the
American Army, I feel sure that the universal feeling
of sadness and regret at their departure, which I found
at Bourges and Tours, would not have been so marked.

"I should like to add that, from my point of view,
this has been one of the most satisfactory units in Queen
Mary's Army Auxiliary Corps, largely due to the sympathy and support which we have received from the
troops serving under you.

"I cannot help feeling that the good understanding
and sympathy which has been established between the
women of Great Britain and the men of the United
States will have a far-reaching effect, and will be the
basis of many life-long friendships."

.   .   .   .   .   .

"I am afraid that I cannot do much actual work,"
Queen Mary had said, with the assumption of her new
title; but, as usual, there were a thousand and one
mothers, sisters, brothers, and more remote relations of
the members of her Corps who decided otherwise.

The Queen's separate post-bag at Buckingham Palace
began to bulge even more alarmingly; and all that
concerned the welfare, physical and moral, of those

fifty-five thousand "Army" women was shifted auto-matically on to Her Majesty's shoulders.

Instantly she was besieged with letters. Frequently the catalogue of woes began with: "My dear Queen Mary," "Dear Queen," and so on; sometimes it ended with the hope that "you will have a good Xmas with the King and family. . . ." And, in spite of the noble efforts of the Controller-in-Chief and her staff, Queen Mary was all too soon overwhelmed with work.

Here again it is the same story; no one knows "how she kept pace with the work; but she did." Her couriers were for ever on route to the Headquarters of the Corps; back and forth from Buckingham Palace the letters flowed in a steady stream.

The new Commandant-in-Chief's brief commen-taries, notes of interrogation and exclamation make reading to-day: here a word of advice appended to a letter received; again a note of condolence or a startlingly practical suggestion. And again is an ex-hortation to treat this "firmly." Something she reads in the newspapers seems to merit, she feels, a "timely rebuke to the administration," whose business it was evidently to see that "this sort of thing did not happen."

"She was unstinting always in her praise; not a single thing seemed to escape her attention; and when it seemed to be found necessary, she gave it to us, straight in the neck!"

Monthly reports of the Corps were subject to the same vigorous scrutiny of the Commandant: "What does this mean?" "This is not clear." There were always hostels to be visited—clubs—sick-beds.

"See to their health; this is most important. . . ."

"In an extraordinary way," I have been told, "she made us personally responsible to her."

And anon would arrive a parcel of pictures and decorative effects to the Controller-in-Chief on the eve of each of her trips to France; for "the Queen felt that the girls might like these pinned up on the walls of their billets to brighten up things for them a little" —pictures, cut from the illustrated papers and carefully pasted on brown paper—amusing cartoons—calendars, and so on. And "Always there was a private message to be conveyed to the girls."

Again, in everything that concerned the Corps one finds evidence of the big vision, the great humanity of Queen Mary, which, having to dispense so often with direct contact, can yet remain so intensely human, so potent with the "personal touch."

"Not a casualty, not a calamity, not a distress was she impervious to: 'May I write the letter of condolence?' or 'Do you think it would come better from Headquarters? . . . Let me know as soon as possible!'"

To the news of some particular deed: "This is a splendid thing. . . . It makes one so proud of our women. . . ."

In the Connaught Club, where the floating population of the Corps passed continually, she moved round in her well-known, encompassing manner; and, of course, like many who had gone before her and not a few who came after, made a bee-line to turn off a certain tap that leaked. . . .

Here again was no mere sympathetic interest, but a grasp, a comprehension of essential points: a shouldering of responsibility, especially for the welfare of the girls who composed the Corps. She had a remedy for every trouble, an idea to meet any new emergency. Nor had the matter to be big and important in order to be met with that alert, ever-readiness of mind. I am reminded of a story Miss Margaret Bondfield has told me of one of the Queen's visits to her headquarters in Park Street in the days of the Central Committee.

In one of the departments there, clothes were made for the needy children of the neighbourhood, and, among the parcels of material for the making of these clothes arrived one day a bulky consignment of furniture fringe. No one could see any possible use for it. "This is beyond me," said Miss Bondfield to the Queen. In a twinkling came the suggestion: "Why not cut off the fringe and use the top for the yokes of serge dresses?" said the Queen.

"Which, of course, was done," added Miss Bondfield, "and served admirably; and it truly was the only conceivable thing to do with such a contribution!"

.   .   .   .   .   .

I cannot well conclude this summary glance at the work of the W.A.A.C. without mention of the splendid pioneer organisation out of which it grew, the Women's Legion, inspired and organised by the Marchioness of Londonderry. Queen Mary had watched the rise and progress of the Legion from its earliest days, when it had centred in Lady Londonderry and Miss Lilian Barker at Woolwich. Out of the Legion grew, in course of time, the more widely known W.A.A.C. organisation.

It was Lady Londonderry who, horrified at the spectacle of the food wasted in so many camps by faulty arrangements and incompetent cooks, had appealed to Sir John Cowans at the War Office to instal women trained under the official military cooks.

The War Office succumbed to repeated representations, and by August 1915, the first hundred cooks, under the ægis of the Women's Legion, were distributed in convalescent camps at Eastbourne and Woodcote Park, Epsom, to correct the appalling food wastage and to release men for service abroad.

The shock of being for the first time dressed in a uniform, to feel, as one of the Legion succinctly summed it up, "like nothing else on earth; and a perfect fool in the bargain," was not the least of the things met by the women who volunteered for the cooking section of the Women's Legion in 1915.

"We worked," said Dame Leach, who was one of them and much later rose to the control of the W.A. A.C.'s, "from six in the morning till eight at night; and for months never saw our billets in daylight, it being before dawn when we left them in the morning and much after dark when we returned at night. . . ."

In 1916 the efforts of the Marchioness of Londonderry and her Legion were officially recognised by an Army Council Instruction; and by this time the Legion's cooks and waitresses were employed in nearly two hundred camps in the United Kingdom.

It was due to the Women's Legion that by 1917, by a further Army Council Instruction, the scheme was further expanded to replace men cooks in France by women, and further: "To effect substitution of women for soldiers in certain employments throughout units, formations, and offices administered by the Army Council. . . . At Home, and at the Bases and on the Lines of Communication Overseas. . . ."

It was the Legion of the Marchioness of Londonderry that made possible the W.A.A.C. organisation; and lived down the first furore of abuse and opprobrium heaped on the heads of women who had the temerity to dress in uniform for the sole reason that a woman so dressed could the better perform her duties. The Legion smiled through months of unspeakable affronts; and eventually thoroughly accustomed the whole country to the sight of uniformed women.

Lady Londonderry has told me: "I once went to lunch at the house of a friend, and, being dressed in uniform, was literally refused admission by the servants in the emphatic belief that I must have come to the wrong house!"

.   .   .   .   .   .

It should be kept well in mind that Queen Mary's "military" associations did not, by any means, begin and end with a woman's army. On July 18th, 1903, when she was Princess of Wales, her name was given to the 18th Hussars, now the 18th Royal Hussars, in grateful recognition of the services rendered by the regiment, and their conspicuous gallantry through the whole of the South African War. Here, actually, Queen Mary's personal military link was forged—a link of which she is, to say the least, extremely proud.

On November 13th, 1910, the designation of the Regiment was changed to the 18th (Queen Mary's

Own) Hussars, and Her Majesty was appointed Colonel-in-Chief.

"Nothing," Colonel Sir Percival Marling, V.C., has told me, "could exceed the interest Her Majesty has always taken in the Regiment; her kindness and generosity to the children and the wives of the N.C.O.'s and men have been beyond words, especially during the Great War, in which the Regiment lost very heavily both in officers and men.

"I once," Sir Percival confessed, "had the honour of staying in the same house for a week with Her Majesty, the house of Lord Tweeddale, my cousin, in Scotland in 1900, when I was invalided home with enteric after Ladysmith. Three or four times I sat next to the Queen at dinner, and she was so friendly and put one so much at one's ease that I almost forgot to say 'Ma'am' by the end of the dinner!"

The pride of the officers and men of the 18th Royal Hussars did not exceed the pride and glory of their Colonel-in-Chief; and the thoughtful act of Her Majesty on August 7th, 1914, before her Regiment departed for France, remained in the memory both of officers and men during the strenuous days that came to them later in France and Flanders.

On the night of August 7th the Officer Commanding the Regiment received a communication from Buckingham Palace to say that Queen Mary intended coming to Tidworth Barracks the next day, and wish her Regiment farewell before it set off to France.

Brigadier-General Burnett has told me:

"The effect of Her Majesty's intimation did much to mitigate the parting from wives, relatives, and friends; and we were especially touched to learn later that the whole conception of the visit emanated entirely from Her Majesty. It inspired us, as few things could have inspired us, for the approaching conflict."

The Regiment was drawn up on the cricket-ground ready for its Colonel-in-Chief's inspection, complete in every detail, fully equipped for France. The men marched past the Queen, halting a few paces from where she stood, and, with their swords in the air, gave her three resounding cheers.

Obviously much moved, the Queen came forward and, in a few eloquent words, told of her pride and her pleasure in the Regiment, and wished them "good-bye" and, from her heart, "God-speed."

It was an affecting ceremony, in which none appeared more moved than the Queen, who then retired to a small enclosure to receive the officers.

Her Majesty wrote many letters to the officers in command of the Regiment in France and Flanders; and the Commander sent regular accounts to Her Majesty of the splendid work of the Regiment, accounts which made the Colonel-in-Chief glow with pride. Chocolates, comforters, cigarettes, arrived in a steady stream from Buckingham Palace, and once, while Colonel Burnett was in London on leave, Queen Mary summoned him to Buckingham Palace so that he might relate personally and in more detail the exploits of the 18th Hussars.

XIX

KNOWING, as one well knows, how entirely alien it is to the spirit of Queen Mary to perform anything in a merely perfunctory way, the more readily does one understand the emotional and nervous stress she suffered during the years of the War from her innumerable visits to the wounded in hospital. It would seem hardly necessary to repeat, were it not for our too easy habit of forgetting, that hardly a single day passed that did not include in the crowded royal schedule a visit to the wounded soldiers.

As a rule, the King and Queen made these visits together; when King George was called away, the Queen undertook the royal visit alone.

That the wounded men themselves derived from the very presence of the King and Queen in their midst a certain sense of personal reward and solace, the thanks of a grateful nation in the inexpressible simple graciousness of Their Majesties has been testified again and again by the doctors and nurses to whose care our wounded men were committed. Always quietly Their Majesties came, often unexpectedly; and in their very inarticulateness on many occasions came the greatest comfort and understanding to the men.

Can one emphasise too much the utter simplicity of Their Majesties as they passed from bed to bed—the elusive, indefinable blending in their attitude of the father and mother who were also King and Queen?

Too often for Queen Mary these visits meant nothing less than an exquisitely protracted torture that would burst from her when she was again home and sunk wearily in a chair, in some such phrase as:

"One felt one could only apologise to the men for being there!"

To such a woman, inhumanly schooled in control, constitutionally incapable of demonstration, most especially on such occasions, the tension at times reached breaking-point; for, over and above her natural sensitiveness, there is in the Queen an acute shrinking from the spectacle of suffering, the sort of fear that often haunts those blessed as she is with superb health and vitality.

It is known by one or two only what a Gethsemane it was for Queen Mary to know of and to witness the long, hopeless illness of her own youngest child, Prince John, who died in his fourteenth year. But this holocaust of Youth she had now daily to witness, in many cases on the day of the soldiers' arrival in hospital with wounds fresh and suffering at its height, touched the gamut of her own suffering. To have been able to render some practical, immediate relief to them, to have herself been in uniform about the wards dispensing balm and the healing touch, would have at least made endurable the harrowing sights.

Not for her these privileges, these compensations; from her was expected the regal presence, the gracious word. Mercifully for Queen Mary, there was much that she could and did do—outside the hospitals; and was it not characteristic that she should entreat the Medical Directors-General of the Admiralty and War Office to move the convalescent men as near as possible to their own homes whenever it was remotely possible?

It was no stereotyped phrase that Her Majesty used as she went from bed to bed; always there was left a sense of personal recognition, of deeds known and marked. There was the quick observation that so quickly noted the nature of the man's wounds, his individual tastes; so that when gifts and presents were to be sent from the Needlework Guild and other organisations, it could be done intelligently, and with some relation to the particular need of those who were to receive them. With "childish glee," it has been said, the wounded men looked forward to the royal visits.

If one lays stress here on the pain Queen Mary underwent in the continual spectacle of human devastation, it does not imply oblivion to the sufferings of the men and youths she visited; and the Queen would be the last person even to admit the agony of those days: rather would she direct attention and sympathy to the men of whom she wrote: "You hold back nothing, and day by day show a love so great that no man can have greater!"

Yet surely there is a time to count the cost to the Queen; to know of the tremblings and terrors her brave words and impassive front so often concealed; to know of the sleepless anxiety that whitened her hair. Through so many a long night was she haunted by the hospital sights of the day; only to rise in the morning with renewed energy and a heart full of prayerful, humble thanks for the practical things at hand to be done—enough of them to tax the brain and hand of a very superwoman.

There is something symbolic of this aspect of Queen Mary's war service in a picture Mrs. Clynes once gave me of her at Windsor sitting on her couch "knitting, knitting, knitting; and never once did she stop the working of those fingers; while she told me how she could not take her mind from the memory of some men she had been visiting who had been 'gassed.' "

The more distressed and agitated she became with the poignant scenes rising up before her eyes, "she knitted faster and faster."

No; she could not forget. "Even the water from their poor eyes scalded the chest it fell on. . . ."

And there would be long silences; and two mothers fixing their eyes on the needles—so grateful for the distraction of the noise of the clicking—until gradually the conversation turned to the socks the Queen was knitting.

"Are they for your boys, Ma'am?"

"Oh dear, no!" Then she added: "They are not for anyone in particular. They go to my Needlework Guild. They are for our soldiers!"

Soon the conversation took a definite turn on the subject of Mrs. Clyne's youngest boy, and a certain toe that was troubling him and keeping him from school.

.   .   .   .   .   .

The practical work of planning, scheming, and organising hospitals for the treatment of wounded soldiers and other Service men undertaken by Queen Mary during the War, apart from, over, and above the more indirect help she rendered, would seem to require a volume in itself.

Here, again, all that one can do is to select individual hospitals out of the many that bear her name, and the even greater number that enlisted her sympathy, interest, and financial support, and endeavour to convey, through them, the value of her work and the spirit in which it was undertaken.

Queen Mary's Roehampton Hospital for Sailors, Soldiers, and Airmen who lost limbs in the War was started by the help of the Queen in 1915; and of the 41,050 odd men who lost limbs in the War, no less than 23,200 of them were treated at the Queen's Hospital, Roehampton, up to December 1924.

Sir Charles H. Kenderdine, K.B.E., Honorary Secretary and Treasurer of Roehampton, on whom devolved so great a burden of the organisation of the hospital in those days of 1915, when Roehampton House was opened with twenty-five beds, concluded to me the epic story of Roehampton and Queen Mary's part in it, in the following words:

"There is no woman I know whose practical knowledge is more comprehensible and intimate than Her Majesty's; whose enthusiasm and interest were so enduring; whose concern was so real; whose advice was so ready; whose help was so invaluable. The combination of her indescribable, exquisite gentleness and strength, and the inspiration this alone afforded to us who were privileged to work with her at Roehampton, is beyond my power to convey."

And Sir Charles but echoes the testimony of all those who have ever worked with the Queen. Miss

Margaret Bondfield was good enough on an occasion succinctly to sum up for me the whole difference between an association with Queen Mary and an association with so many nominal heads of social endeavours and voluntary public servants, the like of which, from Miss Bondfield's emphasis and conviction, I should imagine she had more than enough first-hand experience. "Her competent understanding," said Miss Bondfield, "her entire sincerity, her utter simplicity, are absolutely unlike the 'sympathetic interest' of so many ladies. With her, you know precisely where you are."

There were few points in the laying-out of Roehampton, the staffing and equipment of the hospital, its progress, growth, and development, that Queen Mary omitted to discuss with Sir Charles Kenderdine. Whether these discussions took place at Roehampton or at Buckingham Palace, there was the same minute concern, the same sweeping grasp, the same complete cognizance of difficulties, disheartenments, and setbacks.

"If she lifted an artificial limb, she would note instantly if it were lighter than a previous make; and the fact that to-day Roehampton may boast that it supplies to the limbless the best instruments that the skill of man can devise, the world over, is," says Sir Charles, "so much due to the impetus and encouragement given by the Queen."

Far more even than the practical help given by Queen Mary to Roehampton (straight she sent them seven thousand pounds from the gifts sent at the celebration of Their Majesties' silver wedding), the time, the trouble, the infinite patience she spent on all the details

of the working of the hospital—more than all these
things was the "spiritual strength and backing she
gave," as Sir Charles Kenderdine has expressed it.

Consider only the matter of the workshops erected at
Roehampton. The Army Council were averse from
the idea of introducing workshops in the hospitals, and
so the men were left to fill the intervals of their days
wondering how on earth they could earn their livings
in the future without a leg, an arm. Well, Queen
Mary erected workshops for them where they might
attend classes and receive the best instruction in commercial training, boot repairing, electrical engineering,
cinema operating, metal fitting, and a dozen and one
other trades and professions. She gave them something
else to think about—something to do. And since Queen
Mary's workshops were started at Brighton Pavilion
hospital, thousands of Service men have started a fresh
way in life in spite of their handicaps.

The story of Roehampton cannot be told without
the story of Queen Mary's Hospital, Sidcup, Kent;
for although these hospitals were two separate institutions, yet they shared many things in common, including the Queen's peculiarly intimate concern and personal help, and the pioneer work of Sir Charles Kenderdine.

The Queen's Hospital, Sidcup, was for the treatment
of service men suffering facial injuries—men with
features blown away by shells, some with half their
faces missing; and because of the blessed humane work
of the devoted band of surgeons and nurses at Sidcup,
with Queen Mary as guardian angel, it is alone possible
to endure the terrible stories of the sufferings of these

men so hideously halted on the threshold of their young manhood or in the prime of their lives.

Before the erection of the Queen's Hospital at Sidcup, "facial" cases had alike been treated at the general military hospitals in Aldershot, where, no provision having been made for the peculiar nature of the men's injuries, there was little comprehension of the psychological effects on the men which resulted from the constant reflection in the mirrors and hospital windows of their unspeakable disfigurement. All this, added to the comparative ignorance which prevailed on the subject of facial surgery at the time, left to such patients, to say the least, precious little hope for the future.

So Sir Charles Kenderdine again appealed to Queen Mary, setting before her the new schemes for a new hospital devoted exclusively to facial surgery and the treatment of injured jaw bones, in which hospital there should be concentrated every modern appliance available for mending the mutilations, away from the congested areas and crowded military hospitals, where the men might be reasonably protected from themselves no less than from misguided if sympathetic visitors and spectators.

Instantly, eagerly, the Queen responded; and with one of her truly splendid, unstinting gestures put her influence at the disposal of the Committee; and when she was diffidently approached to know if the Committee might appeal for the name of her daughter, Princess Mary, Viscountess Lascelles, for the hospital, said:

"No; call it after me."

The expectation of the Committee being more than exceeded, and with an immediate, tremendously generous donation from the Queen from a fund placed at her disposal, the hospital was erected in the most beautiful surroundings in Sidcup, in less than six months, at the cost of £149,000 approximately; while the funds contributed to augment the donations of the Queen, and including a gift of £10,000 made by Sir Heath Harrison, Bt., rose to £213,000.

For the soldiers so grievously mutilated, this new order of things, this new atmosphere and skilful attention, was very much a paradise beyond their wildest dreams in the days past when they had hid themselves furtively in corners from the continual reminder of their disfigurements inevitably engendered in the more general hospitals.

Here it was, on her frequent visits, that the "ineffable sweetness and gentleness" of Queen Mary, as they called it at Sidcup, was freely expressed. By March 1919 there were a thousand beds in the hospital, filled not only with the English patients, but with patients from every Colonial Contingent—Canadian, Australian, New Zealand—by arrangement with the Medical Officers in charge of the Overseas Contingents, who speedily realised the value of the new hospital.

Sir Charles Kenderdine has told me that "Her Majesty never missed a single bed" on her visits to Sidcup; and usually exceeded the scheduled time her visit should occupy "by two or three hours. She shrank from nothing. I do not think that it would have occurred to us to withhold certain sights from her. There was that something in her whole attitude and bearing which would have made such a thing simply unthinkable."

With the knowledge that we now have of the Queen's acute sensitiveness to the spectacle of mutilation, the testimony of Sir Charles and the rest of that august, devoted company at Sidcup has a more intense interest for us. It remains to be said that few people outside of the facial hospital, Sidcup, can have any adequate idea of the horrors that there were daily to be seen; of the permanent and incalculable benefit rendered to the men so grievously disfigured; or of the value to scientific research in the plaster casts and pictorial records in the museum attached to the hospital.

. . . . . .

It is a far cry from Sidcup to Stratford, East, where, in the very heart of "Red" London, Queen Mary's Hospital for the East End, tucked away out of sight, little known beyond the borders of Silvertown and the Tidal Basin, dispenses the quiet benedictions of the Queen to the remote districts of East and West Ham, to the farthermost parts of Leytonstone, Plaistow, Forest Gate, and the extremities of Whitechapel; yet the story of the East End hospital does seem to make an excellent and appropriate footnote to Sidcup and Roehampton, standing, as it does, a monument of tangible evidence to the fact that to the humane mind of Queen Mary there is no class, no party, where human want and suffering are concerned: there is only the fact of the suffering and the need of alleviation.

Queen Mary's Hospital for the East End is known familiarly as "Ma's Place," taking its title from a little

conversation that once ensued between Mr. Will
Thorne, Labour M.P. for Plaistow, and H.R.H. the
Prince of Wales at the dinner-table of 4 St. James's
Place, with Lady Astor, the member for the Sutton
Division of Plymouth, as hostess.

The Prince and Will Thorne were seated next to
each other at table, when the member for Plaistow
announced that he had "just come from visiting my
daughter in hospital."

"Oh, I am sorry," said the Prince, with his usual
quick sympathy. "Which hospital is she in?"

Mr. Thorne stared incredulously: "Which hospital?
Why, your Ma's place, of course."

Blank astonishment in the face of the Prince.

"You mean to say you don't know about your Ma's
hospital, Stratford, East?"

And Mr. Will Thorne, it might be added, has been
guilty of less altogether felicitous originalities.

In 1916, during the War, Queen Mary became patron of the Stratford Hospital, of which her son, Prince
Henry, is now President. In 1861 the hospital was
known as The Dispensary, Romford Road. By 1917
the hospital was incorporated by Royal Charter; the
Margaret Lyle Maternity Home was added the same
year—"the finest maternity home" he had seen, said
King George: and "Ma's Place" has appropriated—
and incorporated—the distinction. In 1921 Theydon
Towers was presented to the hospital as a children's
convalescent home.

There is a moving appropriateness about "Ma's
Place"; it is such an eloquent, quiet gesture, so thoroughly characteristic of Queen Mary that, for all her

vigorous repudiation of the trouble makers and tub-thumpers in the Trades Union and Labour Movements, she should so easily, so competently find a meeting-place with them in their sickness and sorrow. It is to "Ma's Place" that the "Reds," their wives and children go for succour and help when things go wrong; "Labour" fills its wards and out-patients' departments; and there the tub-thumpers thump on, even in their delirium.

Among the obstreperous and vociferous patients admitted was one more loquacious even than the rest, more intolerant than the usual. And everyone, even to the patient nurses, wearied of his propaganda. The rest of the ward, among whom were those who did not share his opinions on royalty and the "West," felt, and from time to time gave expression to, the feeling that, when all "had been said and done," it "didn't seem right" that he should "carry on" as he was in the habit of "carrying on"; that if he couldn't be more "perlite," at least he could "shut up"—for the time being, while he remained in the hospital.

One day the Queen suddenly arrived on the scene—her approach unheralded, as usual. She roamed at large over the hospital, and on the part of patients and nurses there was no little trepidation when she came into the "Roberts" ward.

Everyone held his breath when, by an extravagance of fate, she selected the bedside of the incorrigible "Red" for her first attentions. In her arms she carried a bunch of red roses, picked from the royal gardens.

"How d'you do?"

"Fine, thanks."

"Could I give you one of these roses?"

The rose changed hands. Her Majesty became conversational:

"Have you ever been to Hampton Court?"

" 'Ampton Court? No."

"Such a wonderful place. I was there yesterday. You really must get better quickly and go. Will you promise me to go?"

" 'Course."

Her Majesty passed on down the ward, far enough to be out of hearing.

"Nurse," came the hoarse voice from the bed, " 'oo was that?"

With revengeful emphasis: "It was the Queen!"

"Well—blimey!"

It is said that "he got altogether well in time, went out of hospital, and to the end of his stay the well of propaganda dried completely up."

The solicitude of Queen Mary, the scrupulous vigil she keeps over each one of her interests, her Argus-eyed alertness are again copiously proved down at Stratford, East. And, while it is for anyone to know the hundred and one evidences of her quick kindliness —such as when she once walked into the Sisters' sitting-room, and, before crossing the threshold, observing that there was no clock, forthwith measured the mantelpiece with her parasol, and sent one the next day—the most moving testimony to her boundless care and generosity is by her decree kept confidential. I am compelled to say, however, with due and proper regard to the trust reposed in me that, as there never lived a patron more utterly guiltless of one single tincture of the Lady

Bountiful, no purse opened more promptly to the bidding of so compassionate a heart.

With this I must leave the hospital and its royal "secrets."

"Ma's Place" has a portrait of Queen Mary generously given by Mr. Frank O. Salisbury, the painter. It depicts Her Majesty without the formality of state dress—a study made to represent her as she appeared in France during the War, a copy of which forms part of the fresco at the Royal Exchange of "Their Majesties' Visit to the Battle-fields."

Mr. Salisbury was about to go to New York for an exhibition of his work; and it was requested that the portrait of Queen Mary should be included as a special feature.

He sent a message to America to the following effect: "I cannot bring a portrait of Her Majesty in full court regalia, but I have one in ordinary dress."

The reply was to the point:

"This is precisely what we want: the Queen as she is."

The Queen as she is!   One cannot help feeling that you must dive deep in Stratford, East, to find the Queen as she most truly is.

XX

AFTERMATH

QUEEN MARY does not forget. The "uncanny memory" about which one hears so much holds vividly—and will no doubt to the end of her days hold —the years of the War: all that they meant to her, all that they taught her.

To the "Sisterhood of your great country," responding to a "word of cheer" addressed to Her Majesty by the Women of America, New Year's Day, 1918, the Queen wrote:

"The horrors of war have taught us to know one another better, and have strengthened the ties of kinship and mutual sympathy by uniting the women of the English-speaking races heart and soul in the struggle for liberty and civilisation. Confident of the valuable help we women can give . . . I pray God's richest blessing on our efforts."

How much more, then, did the "horrors of war" strengthen the "ties of kinship" between the noble patriot and the women of her own country?

How could she, of all women, ever forget her debt and the debt of her countrywomen to: "The men of our Army, Navy, and Air Force," to whom, in April 1918, from Windsor Castle she sent that wonderful message:

". . . Our pride in you is immeasurable, our hope unbounded, our trust absolute. . . . You are offering your all. You hold back nothing, and day by day you show a love so great that no man can have greater.

"We, on our part, send forth with full hearts and unfaltering will the lives we hold most dear. . . . In God's name we bless you, and by His help we, too, will do our best."

Mark, in these words, the ring of the woman that is Queen Mary!

Being impressed as, I think, no one can fail to be impressed by the strength, the simplicity, and the beauty of language in the few messages that go forth from the Queen to the nation, I once asked someone working close to Her Majesty if the phrasing, as well as the thought and feeling they contained, came undiluted from her pen; and was assured most heartily that in phrasing, thought, and feeling the messages come straight from the Queen!

War passes, but the service of Queen Mary goes on, will go on until the end. Still hers the "privilege," did she not call it, in her message to the women of the British Empire in December 1918—the "high privilege of service"?

Of those women she wrote also to the world preparing for peace:

"They have risen to the great opportunity, and have proved their courage, steadfastness, and ability. . . .

"My heart is full of admiration and gratitude for what I have seen. . . .

"A new era is dawning upon the world, bringing with

it many difficulties, fresh responsibilities, and serious problems to be faced. . . .

"To-day, more than ever, the Empire needs her daughters, for in the larger world of public and industrial work women are daily taking a more important place.

"As we have been united in our work, whether of head or hands, in a real sisterhood of suffering and service during the War, let us go on working together with the same unity of purpose for the settlement and reconstruction of our country."

As ever, the Spartan ring: Settlement—Reconstruction; with Courage—Steadfastness—Ability.

The laurels of the War that came to Queen Mary were the "high privilege" still to Serve.

During the War her hair whitened. To-day they tell you: "It but lends further distinction to her presence; still more regal does she look."

Yet what of her heart when she looked over the war-stricken world and over "My beloved country"?

She speaks of Courage—Steadfastness—Unity, and in the deep, measured language of the Prayer Book: "Above all, for this holds all other loyalties together, loyalty to God."

It is recorded of the solemn ceremony to the Unknown Warrior buried in Westminster Abbey:

"More pathetic than any was the sight of Queen Mary, who, as the King moved to sprinkle the sacred soil of France over the grave of the Unknown Warrior, seemed to break in her sorrow. . . . Queen Alexandra took her comfortingly by the arm as she wept. . . ."

These "indulgences" are indeed rare with Queen

Mary.   It is not by tears or by much talk that she remembers the desolation of youth she witnessed daily in the war hospitals; nor the clutchings of the children in the crèches whom she picked up to comfort as they wept for fathers in Flanders and mothers working in some canteen kitchen, though the memory of these things serve as an eternal reminder.

Like most people, she shrinks from recalling the War; but in looking to the Future, she remembers the Past.   Her work in these days is instinct with the memory of the War.

And one does not marvel that now her impatience is so much greater with idle wasters; that when she is confronted in a weekly illustrated paper with the spectacle of some of our "idle rich" abandoning themselves on some fashionable sea-shore in France in gossamer attire, there is such withering scorn in her: "They would look almost more decent if they had no clothes on at all!"

Again, when she is petitioned to sanction the publication in the newspapers the descriptions of her dresses because, she is informed, "people like to know about these things," the petition is summarily dismissed, and later renewed—with added ardour by those who share a reflected glory in these things.   Her Majesty is reminded that it is now customary for ladies to make their sartorial effects in the evening also a sensation in the morning's news.   The retort is brief and to the point: "So much the worse, then, for our social life!" And later: "It does seem to me not only ostentatious and unnecessary display, but so thoughtless, too.   Imagine being hungry or out of work, and continually confronted with accounts of other people's luxury and pleasure. . . ."

They have cause to know, who work near to Queen Mary, how much she remembers; how that in service to the Now, in keeping her eyes fixed on the Future, she best remembers.

To say, in these post-war days, that Queen Mary is one of the hardest-worked women in her realm is almost to be guilty of a platitude. Even those sequestered souls of Lambeth whose pride it is that they have never crossed Westminster Bridge have long suspected it, yet none know better than those who work closest with the Queen how difficult a thing it is to define Her Majesty's work—as difficult as to define how much of life is left to her outside of her service.

"While in many ways," I have been told, "the King is a 'specialised' worker, with 'office hours' that might intimidate a man of Big Business, it is almost impossible to specify the nature of the Queen's work."

To many the magnitude of the Queen's service comes as a sudden realisation, most startling, most disconcerting.

When, for example, she visited the Mary Macarthur Memorial Home, Ongar, in July 1924, the late Mr. Fred Bramley, who also was present, watching the Queen, turned aside and whispered fervently to a friend:

"We must certainly pass a new law for Queens to limit their hours of work."

When Her Majesty went to Shoreditch in March 1922 to learn for herself of the housing conditions, to see the tumble-down streets which it was piously hoped to replace with cottages and flats, and Shoreditch turned out in its thousands, it sounded "strange" to the ears of those who do not often go East to hear the waiting ladies of Shoreditch opine that "The Queen— Gawd bless 'er—works as 'ard as any. . . ."

It is true; however, there may be exceptions to this instinctive conviction—like the lady of Putney who wrote with fluent forcefulness to Queen Mary belabouring her for the "good time you've been having at Ascot" (alas that the lady could not know Queen Mary's feelings on many an enforced social occasion, particularly on the racecourse, for she would indeed be startled).

To the Queen comes so little respite. "Then Your Majesty must not stand so much. You must sit down more, Ma'am . . ." she was firmly told on an occasion by one of her medical advisers.

Afterwards Queen Mary turned to someone also present in the room, and said, with her whimsical smile: "I must not stand so much. Too funny!"

The appeals that come to Queen Mary, public and private, are endless; and whether the letter is addressed to "Mrs. Queen," "Mrs. England," "Madam Majesty" (it is simply amazing how the changes are rung on the form of address) they are all alike opened by Queen Mary; for she attends to her own post.

Private devotions over, her public day begins; and mostly, it is all day. Before breakfast, beginning actually with the hair-dressing, the back of the post is broken; and on each letter are pencilled directions for the reply.

It is a remarkable as well as a colossal post that comes

to Her Majesty at Buckingham Palace; and sandwiched
in the multifarious appeals is sometimes a delightful,
to Her Majesty inspiring and encouraging, little note,
lovingly laboured, possibly from somewhere in the Isle
of Dogs:

"Just a few lines hoping you are the same as it leaves
me at present. . . . Wishing your son the Prince of
Wales many, many happy returns of the day, God bless
him. . . . I shall always remember your son's birthday, for he was born on my wedding day. . . ."

"So kind of her to remember my David. . . ."

It brings swiftly the inexpressible smile; and there
are more letters, scores of them; but still there was the
homely little note from the Isle of Dogs!

How wonderful Queen Mary is simply in the matter of dealing with her vast correspondence is a
commonplace at Buckingham Palace. She postpones
nothing. The attention claimed is given at once. Immediately, too, is the decision made. Nothing is set
aside; and there is no to-morrow.

Like the capable head of a great business house, she
works carefully, with precision and promptitude. There
is about it all a thoroughly "masculine" economy—a
bigness, an air of: Let us proceed to the next point—
after she has clipped the trimmings, if any, from a
letter submitted, or more pointedly re-phrased a para-
graph. The motion is always forward, with no looking
back at a thing settled yesterday; and Buckingham
Palace has not always been so businesslike in its business dealings inside and outside the Palace.

There is no glorified attention to detail; but let the

detail relate to some human being, and then the Queen is "relentless."

Her values in such details I may perhaps best illustrate by an incident that occurred not long ago when an Englishwoman, living in a remote French village, appealed to the Queen in a distress that was agitating her. It was not enough that her distress should be relieved instantly from the private purse of her Queen. Back and forth from Buckingham Palace letters went to every English institution or association that could possibly be discovered in the vicinity; for to Queen Mary the suppliant must have not only monetary relief, but the opportunities of contact and company, if she would wish to avail herself of these things. And, finally, there must be someone to stand by, as it were, and relieve such distresses as might possibly occur in the future. The sheer detail that Queen Mary attended to in this particular instance, the sources she stirred up, her encompassing panacea, leaves the lady-in-waiting who acted as emissary for the Queen still gasping with surprise. Detail! Yes, when it is related to the human, the personal.

Her way of giving presents, for example. Of someone it is asked, What can we give him?

"Well, I know that he smokes cigarettes by his fingers. Let us give a cigarette-case. . . ."

(I should apologise, and do, for intruding anything so crude as this explanation of the extravagant reputation that the Queen has with her various household staffs for somehow so mysteriously knowing "what a man wants.")

. . . . . .

In Queen Mary's appeal to the women of the Empire, December 1918, that with her they should continue the "sisterhood of service and sacrifice" engendered by the War, in facing the new problems and responsibilities that came with the peace, she specifically mentions the causes of Education and Housing.

"It always seemed to me that poverty really hurts the Queen," Mrs. Clynes once told me; and there are truly few sights that can reduce her to more abject misery than the sight of a broken-down, decrepit-looking house. When all has been said, who should know better than Queen Mary the value and the power of a home in its influence on the lives of the men and children who must live there? Has she not always, in all things, first seen that her own house was in order? Is she not married to an Englishman who would rather sit in his own home than do anything else in the world; who insists on his own fireside and its inviolability; who finds contentment and repose alone there?

In March 1922 Queen Mary spent a Saturday afternoon in Shoreditch, accompanied by Lady Cynthia Colville (who has done so much in the local maternity work), Mr. Harry Verney, and Lady Ampthill. Shoreditch turned out gallantly and in full force to do honour to the royal visitor.

Ten deep the crowds of Cockneys stood and gave the Queen a welcome that she would find hard to forget. She was deeply moved by the spontaneity and warmth of the people—emotions that must have mingled oddly with others aroused by what she saw in the homes in which they lived.

In Wilmer Gardens, where the housing conditions

of so many parts of the East End of London may be seen in all their sordidness, a chivalric effort had been made to hide broken window-panes and other evidence of the desolation and destitution there prevailing by nailing up every picture of the royal family that could be found in Shoreditch—and not the least of the shocks that awaited Queen Mary was the ramification of "dated" pictures of her family.

Round and about Ware Street she toured in her characteristic way, and when she turned at last despairingly to a woman of Ware Street and asked, "Why, why do you live here?" was reminded with firm courtesy that it was because "We can't git nowhere else, Ma'am."

The royal visitor departed, leaving Wilmer Gardens to pass a unanimous verdict that "in one way and another she had as 'ard a time as us, and did as much work." They were impressed by her simple genuineness and rejoiced at least in her heartfelt sympathy; for once or twice during the visit Her Majesty had forcibly expressed her opinion of the conditions, and these opinions sped like wildfire round the neighbourhood.

Shoreditch, it would seem, had a good time. The Queen returned to Buckingham Palace—and her reflections.

Of Lady Cynthia Colville I recently asked the not unnatural question: "But what did it all come to—beyond Her Majesty's expressions of horror; what did Her Majesty DO?"

"I suppose nothing, directly," was the reply; "but then direct action is not possible from the Queen. . . . The impetus her visit gave, however, was incalculable.

One of the results was the forty thousand pounds voted within the next week or two by the London County Council toward clearing up the horror."

With the knowledge, then, of the significance of the Queen's presence alone, consider how unstintingly she has bestowed that presence in the plague-spots of London!

Is not the catalogue of her post-war slum tours endless? From Woolwich to Kensington she has gone indefatigably, from the poor babies in the crèches of Deptford to the public wash-houses in Kensington, where poor women workers "rest" from their labours through the week scrubbing the family clothes at the wash-tubs on Saturday afternoon.

To Hampstead Her Majesty has been, and to Bethnal Green, soon after she heard from the Mayor of the conditions of the slum property in the Brady Street area. With the Prince of Wales she toured the Duchy properties of Kennington to "look over the land" and give "practical help and advice."

She has spared no effort, and, knowing the value of the very presence of the Queen, every effort was made to secure her presence—except perhaps at Poplar, thanks to Mr. George Lansbury, one of the oldest of the Board of Guardians at Poplar, who "insisted" on giving the Queen a "change"—a chance to see brighter Poplar in the form of the Poor Law Schools at Shenfield, Essex, where many poor children of Poplar are really well cared for.

It should never be forgotten that for all the power, virtual and actual, of the Consort of the King of Great Britain, Emperor of India, she is rigorously precluded from doing much in the power of the least housewife who cares to exert herself enough to work locally on some committee or Board of Guardians. Queen Mary, for all her great opportunities, has no such privilege. She is simply not permitted personally to identify herself with schemes and projects, which are the privileges of commoners.

That she makes no attempt to conceal her plans, ideas, and sympathies in the matter of Housing and Education is well known to the heads of these ministries, with whom she confers frequently and with mutual profit. Within the limitations rigorously imposed on her she works ceaselessly; and it is well always to keep in mind the war-time service of Queen Mary, when her activities were not so sharply proscribed.

Her Majesty's "private" enterprises in housing, which may be seen in many rows of cottages erected on the Sandringham estates (where her husband is the landowner, and she is as free to work as any squire's wife), most excellently set forth her creed that the labourer is not only worthy of his hire, but that his wife and children also are worthy of clean, decent, comfortable homes.

It is strictly true of Queen Mary that the care of the cottages on her husband's estates is to her a matter no less important than the care of her own home; the education of the children of agricultural labourers of no less import to the country than was the education of her own children.

Queen Mary's attitude towards the education of her own sons and daughter was only a part of her attitude towards education in general, with an added sense of the need of a certain specialisation to fit them for the posts they would be called on to fill.

The Queen believes in Youth—trusts it, has pride in it, and, as befits one who lodges so great a faith and confidence in Youth, is not content with little from it. Here again is she extraordinarily unsentimental; and it is a fact that often she stands singularly alone in her belief in Youth, where others are full of suspicion and distrust. This pride in her children, this hope and expectation, to which must be added what Mrs. Clynes has called the "quality of her motherliness," illumine her attitude to her own children and the children of the nation.

For her faith in her children and for her trust, though not for these things alone, does Queen Mary evoke a rare confidence and devotion from her children; and as one who watched them grow up has remarked to me: "They are only too like all other children in that the older they grow the more do they realise their debt to their mother."

If in the matter of the education of her children Queen Mary had not the last word, the influence of her "attitude" was ever strongly felt. She stood unrelenting for an all-round education for each one of them, strengthened in her stand by the knowledge of the stupidities perpetrated so often in the education of princes who preceded her own sons. She was uncompromising about their lessons. Again, there was always "Mamma's" intelligence to reckon with; which seldom faltered, as did neither her tranquillity nor her reliableness. These things were always with her, and were always felt by her children. It *was* hard to be stupid or slack with her!

The King and Queen once stopped in the schoolmaster's house on the Sandringham estate, where mine host, having knowledge of and great regard for the antiquities of his native place, proudly showed his visitors a prehistoric remnant lately excavated in his garden.

"What sort of an animal is that?" asked the King. "Anything in the nature of a snipe?"

"Why, no," said the Queen, modestly hazarding a piece of abstruse archæological information on a cursory examination of the strange object. And she was found to be quite correct.

The children were brought up in Spartan simplicity, of course; and with such unpretentious parents it would have been hard for them to grow up other than "natural." No father watched with more ecstatic eagerness the arrival of his children into the world, nor lavished a more exuberantly abundant devotion on them.

Parental joys were delightfully shared with those who nursed the children and saw to their earliest instruction. The attitude of the King and Queen on this point was reflected in King George's remark to the village schoolmaster when he expressed his gratitude at being invited to Windsor for the ceremony of the Confirmation of "David":

"Well, after all, you were his first teacher!"

The sympathy, the understanding, the great attachment which exists between "David," her first-born, Prince of Wales, and his mother is remarked by all who know it. It is a strong and deep feeling, and, like all such feelings, admits of little sentiment or public demonstration. To "David," as to them all, "Mamma" is "always there"—a rock and a bulwark.

"The business of constancy," said Montaigne, "is bravely to stand-to;" and the greatest of mothers are eminently accomplished in this when their children come of age to assume their own responsibilities and find their own selves. To such mothers it is "always such a Godsend to come home again," as the Prince of Wales said to his first schoolmaster when he returned to the calm of Sandringham at the close of the War.

Those who watched the ceremony of the investiture of the Prince of Wales to the most noble Order of the Garter at Windsor Castle in 1911 will not easily forget, among other emotions of that day, the pride in the face of Queen Mary as, hand in hand with the King, she walked behind "David," in her Garter robe over a sapphire gown, her fair hair under its quaint velvet covering glinting in the sunshine, as though catching the gleam of the sunlight as it fell on the fair-haired boy who went before. Nor will they easily forget the mother, with her heart almost leaping out of her eyes, watching every step of the pale, awed "David," as, preceded by Garter Black Rod, his hat surmounted with large plumes of white ostrich and black heron, looking neither to the right nor to the left but straight into his mother's eyes, he entered the throne-room to make obeisance to the King and Queen.

And when the stately ritual—which has endured more than five hundred years since the days when it was established by Edward III, and renewed in all its ancient splendour by King George V at the investiture of the Prince of Wales—was over, there were two visible expressions of relief: one on the face of the Prince when he removed his tall plumed hat before entering the Chapel, the other on the face of his mother.

.   .   .   .   .   .

To select only one tangible evidence of the Queen's post-war "memory," yet another of her private enterprises, one need go no farther than Hampstead, to the model Maternity Home which bears her name, "for the wives and children of men who are or have been serving with His Majesty's Forces." Here is an unfettered expression of her thoughts and feelings about the mothers of the nation and the treatment they should have—where (I quote from the letters of a nurse who worked there) "I feel as all must feel, that to be in such an atmosphere magnifies the joy of service; for the spirit of happiness hovers everywhere and seems to penetrate the farthest corner."

Her Majesty's interest in babies has been much talked of in the past; what is not so well known, I think, is that it is not so much the "adorable bundles of helplessness" that appeal to her, as the potential men and women they are. Her attitude is notably unsentimental, and, as is very evident at Hampstead, her concern is equally divided between mother and child.

The Maternity Home was started by Queen Mary; it continues with her support, augmented by a devoted band of women, nurses, doctors, of whom (I quote from the letter of a patient) "we cannot speak too highly for all the kindness, the attention, and the love we had under your care. . . . We shall never be able to repay you for what we have had."

May I digress to say how one is impressed by the gratitude of the Service men whose wives are tended at Hampstead.

"If ever I hear it said that nothing is being done for the Service men, I shall always remember, and I shall always remind people of, Queen Mary's Maternity Home, Hampstead."

And again, in the fullness of a grateful heart: "I have taught my little lads to raise their hats when they pass a Catholic church. And now we shall also always raise them when we pass 'Queen Mary's.' "

There is so much of Queen Mary in her Maternity Home, Hampstead. She raised it first as an "enduring memorial to the efforts of many women of the Empire who gave their aid to the common cause during the War." The impetus came from the deep impression always made on the Queen by the spectacle and by the knowledge of the terrible amount of avoidable suffering and loss of life arising so often from maternity and motherhood that is without humane and adequate medical and nursing facilities.

Queen Mary felt, as always she has felt, that at such a time a woman needs individual care—the individual care she would receive in her own home did the means and circumstances permit—freedom from all anxiety, peace, and a sense of security.

These things the humanitarian set out to achieve in her own Maternity Home, which she hoped would serve as a model for other charitably minded women to follow all over the country.

That the "Home" should be small enough to suggest a home was her first rule laid down; and then she made it a condition that no mother should leave the Home in less than three weeks after the birth of her child, knowing, as Queen Mary well knew, what a temptation it was to most working women to return too soon to work.

In the face of certain doubts and diffidences Queen Mary insisted that a wing should be added to the Home to which the expectant mother might bring her youngest child to be cared for, as the mother herself was to be cared for; and thus greatly mitigate the mother's worry and anxiety on account of leaving her youngest child at home. The Queen was firm on this point; and the new wing was added.

To conclude the fundamental principles laid down by the Queen at the inception of the Home, I must mention that she decreed also that no effort should be spared, before the mother left Hampstead, to teach her at least the elements of modern mothercraft and infant care, so that the good work might be continued in her own home.

Dame Florence Leach has told me that the Queen once expressed to her an aversion for mottoes. There is, however, an unwritten motto at Hampstead, namely: "Every woman to be treated as if she were the Queen."

Certainly the spirit of the Queen is everywhere over the Home. There is nothing perfunctory; everything matters—as it has from the beginning, when the Queen must be consulted even on the patterns of the curtains to be put up. She acutely cares, and will have no "red tape."

"If the soldiers WANT fifty thousand socks, then send them straight from the Friary," she said one day at the Needlework Guild headquarters. "What THEY want is all that matters." This gesture at "officialdom" too imposing is characteristic.

It is so at Hampstead. It is the mother that matters, and the child; for them the Home exists. And so, coming into a ward, her eye lights swiftly on a bed where "This patient can be seen from the window. This will never do. . . ." Again: "There are no shades on these lights. It will hurt their eyes to lie in bed with unshaded lights."

At the ceremony of the opening of the new permanent Home (it was started at Cedar Lawn, Hampstead, in 1919, removed to the permanent building in 1922 on a site given by the late Lord Leverhulme) the real autocrats of the press, the photographers, would be appeased by nothing less than a picture of the Queen holding a baby; and into the Queen's arms one of the babies was placed.

Instantly Queen Mary's voice was heard: "Matron! But what is the matter with its eye?"

"It was as if she had gone into her own nursery and at once detected a slight inflammation on the baby's eyelid."

The photograph shows the look of deep concern on the Queen's face, with the matron bending over also examining the child; and it was all rather unfortunate on the press photographers. . . .

"A trivial incident, you may think," said Miss Edith Manning, O.B.E., concluding her story, "but it does seem to tell a lot."

XXI

"THEREFORE it is," says Montaigne, "that to make a right judgment of a man you are chiefly to pry into his common actions and surprise him in his everyday habits."

So often I have heard the plaintive note from those who see most of the "everyday habits" of Queen Mary, those who, by necessity, are farthest removed from that strange lustre which envelops queens and hides them from us:

"If only we might show her as she really is!" (A pious hope which, they believe, can never be fulfilled.)

The revealing, for example, of her sheer humanness in her "common actions," which perhaps alone explains why the most beloved of her ladies always left her with:

"Goodnight, darling Ma'am!"

It makes and keeps her simple; it is the only explanation of her genius in human relationship—this so great humanness. It is why there is only one way to the Queen, one appeal—the simple, the natural.

Stand on ceremony, and she can become more stiffly ceremonial than a Master of Ceremonies, and in the presence of formality be easily metamorphosed to a monument of the grimly formal.

It is said that she does not "go out" easily to meet people; and possibly it is because most people perforce feel that they must always be "dressed up" to meet her, leaving nothing to the simple of the earth. Of course the smart tradeswoman conducts her whole interview in a series of gasps, in a perpetual state of flutter; and Queen Mary can talk from a peak on Olympus as well, if not better, than the next one.

There was, however, the new fitter who came to pin some garments on the Queen, "rather agitated, it being the first morning of her new experience." This agitation she had pathetically confided to one to whom familiarity with the royal presence had lent perfect ease. The fitter was enjoined to be "quite, quite natural" when she "went down to the Presence"— and struggled so desperately hard to be "quite, quite natural" that "before she had fixed the fourth pin she trembled all over." The more entirely naturally Queen Mary conducted the conversation, the more the fitter trembled and shook.

"By the time it was all over," said the cool observer, "it would be difficult to say who was trembling the more —the fitter or the Queen!"

Again, when "David" brought his devotions to "Mamma" in the form of an onyx brooch just before Their Majesties left for Italy after the King's indisposition some months ago. When the Prince had departed, "Mamma" sat "surrounded with farewell gifts in every shape and form," but oblivious to everything but the little onyx brooch.

"So good of David to think of me! So good of him! . . ." Then the excited: "But where can I put it? I must wear it." And finally, they found a place in the front of her toque to which the onyx brooch was duly pinned, and "Mamma" left London for Italy in the seventh heaven of joy.

"Georgie's" bouquet awaited her in Paris when she returned from Italy through France; and altogether there seemed no end to the good things of life.

Serenity—poise. There is much of these qualities in the "everyday" manners of the Queen; she is sparing of emphasis, and does not use the superlative degree. Those who know her best can count on their fingers the occasions of her outbursts. Once they happen they are not easily forgotten, as when at York Cottage, more than a decade ago, she once stamped her foot at someone and said: "How dare you!"

Again, during the War, when the state of our domestic politics had reached a pitch of confusion that seemed to spell disaster, she cried:

"Oh, for a week of those days when *we* could do something!"

For the most part, however, she moves serenely through the day and, when it is necessary, can suffer fools with tremendous patience and dignity. It is her highly developed sense of proportion that gives her poise.

No one is familiar with her: which would seem to reflect little on the innate dignity of a queen, not exposed, as Queen Mary has been considerably exposed, to motley crowds and strange assemblies coming in the trail of a political party at Court that rates finesse and the elegance of the courtier very much below par.

"You think me punctilious in Her Majesty's presence?" Mary Macarthur once answered the chal-

AN INFORMAL SNAPSHOT OF THE QUEEN

THE LATEST STUDIO PORTRAIT OF THE QUEEN

lenge of a critic. "You do not know the woman she is. One does not take liberties with her!"

It is so; and Queen Mary had rubbed shoulders with much rugged heartiness since the days of the War and, on the whole, can be said really to relish it!

"How I like the man! I believe he is genuinely concerned for the workers!" And, after all, what else mattered? Yet, as the rough-hewn who have gone to Court are first to testify, always she preserves that "certain strangeness," is guilty of stateliness more often than excessive fellowship, and does not scatter indiscriminately the myrrh and rosemary of her sweetness and smile. And they like it; confident that with her, the absence of heat and haste indicates the finer qualities of depth of sincerity.

Said Keir Hardie once of Queen Mary: "When that woman laughs, she does laugh, and not make a contortion like so many royalties!"

There is real fun in Queen Mary: she has the gift of genuine laughter and light-heartedness; and the housemaid newly promoted to the upper regions of Buckingham Palace was taken "all aback" to hear whistling coming down a corridor, where, she had assumed, one did not hear such things—and she did not at all "approve" of the Queen's whistling snatches from musical comedies.

You may catch the fun in a glint of the blue eyes as when, for example, she endeavoured to describe a cup of tea she had been given and fell back vaguely on the assertion that "It was simply a funny old cup of tea."

There is, too, her humour—appreciative rather than provocative—and her flights in theatricals. Mary

Moore bears testimony to this; for when she and Sir Charles Wyndham once gave a "command" performance of *David Garrick* at Windsor Castle before King Edward and were afterwards summoned to the King, Mary Moore found Queen Mary, then Princess of Wales, giving a first-rate rendering of Mrs. Gorringe in *Mrs. Gorringe's Necklace*. This was a part created by Lady Wyndham in the eighties and a favourite of Queen Mary's in those days, when with her mother and brothers she was often to be seen in a box at the Criterion. (*Still Waters Run Deep* was a particular favourite of H.R.H. the Duchess of Teck; Queen Mary's taste was for light and musical plays.)

It may be that no man is a hero to his own valet; but I would commend you to those who stitch and sew for Queen Mary really to know of her exquisite courtesy and humanness.

It is not extravagance to say that Queen Mary is literally adored by the women who work for her in the matter of dress. Not that this branch of the royal service is at all easy, for such a mixture is the Queen of pliancy and sheer immovableness on the subject of her clothes: which is to say that she will have what she wants, and least of all qualities that those who "dress ladies" are accustomed to is, apparently, decision—definiteness.

The tears shed alone on her preference for toques in millinery—because she is "accustomed" to toques! And because in a toque she feels more comfortable— as though you could ever make a woman look attractive and comfortable at the same time! However, it must be comfortable; so not an eighth of an inch will she endure it lower on her eyes! She is adamant.

Of her ankles, of her feet—perfect as plaster casts—the shoemakers, and others, rave; yet she will not tolerate a glimpse of an ankle—again entirely suiting her own sense of suitability!

If Queen Mary is "unclever about clothes," inasmuch as she will not endure "horrible tassels that get in my way everywhere I turn"; or the most "too, too, gorgeous coat" that will hinder her movements ("My dear girl, *can* you see me getting out of a carriage with all this round my feet?"); if she will be comfortable rather than *chic*, and is stubbornness personified where her requirements are involved—she could not be said to be indifferent either to her clothes or to her appearance. On the contrary. Her sartorial "idiosyncrasy," as it has been called, is only another expression of her acute feeling for harmony. If she changes a gown, then the adornments worn with the last are also changed unless they are each one meticulously in keeping; and nothing would induce her to introduce the suspicion of a "dressy" element in walking or sport attire.

Her favourite colour in dress is a wistaria-delphinium blue—pale, soft, with a suggestion of mauve in the blue—Pervenche blue; just as in furnishing she leans to Du Barry rose, or, as it has been called, that shade nearest approaching the colour of dead rose-leaves. In all things she prefers soft pastel shades to brilliancy in colouring. She has a marked aversion to black—so marked, in fact, that women in mourning have not appeared at Court until their time of mourning was over.

It would seem scarcely necessary to say that Queen Mary is not intimidated by the caprices of Fashion; the clothes she wears are fashioned by her own tastes and preferences. Her dislike of imitations in place of the genuine brocade, silk, satin—as the case may be—is notorious, and as she is able to indulge her passion for the real material, she has always done so.

When the outcry against women wearing ospreys was raised some years ago while Queen Mary was Princess of Wales, representations were made to her, as indeed to all other royal ladies of the Court, to sign a pledge not to wear these adornments secured at such cruel cost to the birds from which they were torn. For some reason not known, the Queen was averse to the actual signing of the petition; but gave her word that she would, in the future, refrain from wearing osprey in any shape or form of adornment. And to this day she has kept her word; while other royal ladies who gaily signed the petition, gaily wore the osprey to the end of their days!

Her Majesty's shrinking from the cheap imitation in so much of fashionable modern clothes does relate to something deep in her character; and it operated from the earliest days at White Lodge, as was abundantly testified to me by one who "dressed" Princess May at that time, the late Mlle. Tatry. There simply is not anything about Queen Mary that is artificial; and this fact is always vehemently brought home to one by those who should know. They speak of her "wholeness" as well as her "wholesomeness" and "exquisite cleanness"—inadequate terms for the most part; but what they lack in fitness is made up in emphasis.

There simply is no fake; no tampering either with her beautiful grey hair or with that enviable complexion, the best expression of her "wholesomeness" and not, as is often assumed, a sublime tribute to some potent cosmetic. There is something frigidly "English" in the entire absence of restoratives and correctives from her toilet-table. It just is so; and it is not the fruits of any theory in the matter. As soon think of commending a thing to Queen Mary on the ground that it would make her look young, as of asking her to tell a lie! It is "not done": she is shockingly truthful!

And the fastidiousness which cannot countenance sham or gaudiness in the matter of clothes recoils also from ostentation at table. Life in the royal household is stately but not luxurious; meals simple, not fantastic and complicated; and the visitor from abroad, spoiled by the sight of so many palaces in Europe and consequently "appalled" by the simplicity in size and architecture of Buckingham Palace, would be even more disagreeably affected to know how harmoniously the inner life there blends with the outward appearance.

. . . . . .

The personalities of the Consorts of Kings of England have always seemed to count so little in history; less notable even than their influence for their Courts was their influence on the lives of their husbands, the Kings.

In the Middle Ages the names of Queen Eleanor and Queen Philippa stand out in picturesque relief. Elizabeth, as a reigning sovereign, and also Queen Victoria, hold a place apart in our chronicles; but most of the wives of our long line of Kings are conspicuous for their utter inconspicuousness.

Then came Queen Mary, the first Queen Consort of English blood since Henry VII united the houses of Lancaster and York by his marriage with Elizabeth, daughter of Edward IV—a modern woman spiritually, intellectually emancipated; while yet retaining in her own person as wife, as mother, and as friend, a fragrance that belongs to times that now seem far off and fugitive.

Greatly here rests the power of Queen Mary—in the Kingdom of her own home—which is an axiom throughout the Empire; holding her sway by virtue of a devotion so absolute, so utterly self-less that those who know it can only say:

"Such devotion we have not seen in any wife."

And the Court, the symbol of the stability, the pivot of English social life, takes its colouring and quality from the home-life of the King and Queen, surviving strongly, splendidly, while nearly every Court in Europe disintegrates and nearly every throne totters and falls.

There is an element in English social life that most emphatically does not borrow its manners from the Court; and so much the worse for England and the particular social set. One is not here concerned with them; but with the women of Queen Mary's Court, holding, as it does, much of the best of British womanhood, each showing and reflecting Queen Mary's eye for character, her intuition for people—her sensitiveness to the "atmosphere" of those who serve her in the most menial capacity, as to her courtiers and ladies.

She has no need to lift her voice to make herself heard; and when a certain lady was in the running for a court post with ancestral recommendations to which even royalty, one would think, could not be impervious, Queen Mary said quietly, finally:

"No; I think not. She is too haughty." It is characteristic.

The Court of the mightiest Empire in the civilised world is small, very small, but it glows and shines with a set of women about whom all too little is heard of home and abroad, each with her record of service, over and above her service to the Queen. Diverse are they in outlook and interest—one here with strong Labour sympathies, another with her schemes of Social Reform in true Victorian tone—all one in their silent devotion to the woman they serve.

I was emboldened on an occasion to ask Lady Mount-Stephen (who had served, too, the Queen's mother) how was engendered this deathless loyalty that Queen Mary so supremely commanded from her friends, that was so disinterested; how came these friendships with so little of "property" in them, yet were they so "personal," that seemed to feed on so little of actual sight and contact, yet were they so deep, unswerving.

"I cannot tell you how utterly untrivial is the Queen. She never fails. It is a luxury to see her; a continued inspiration just to know always that she *is*."

Yet again, to a woman of fashion, one of the smartest of the "smart set," who conceals more natural brains and abilities than I have met in a woman beneath an unruffled social charm; a critical, spirited, fearless woman, I asked the question.

"Whatever happens," she said, "you just know that the Queen would never 'let you down.'"

What can one say of the incredibly shy, sensitive soul who compels such devotion in spite of her almost constitutional inability to "go out" to people?

On her tour of India at her husband's side, at a garden party given in honour of the royal visitors, Queen Mary was greatly attracted to a pretty child also at the party.

They exchanged compliments, and Queen Mary, amused by the child's demeanour, said, gently challenging:

"You don't know who I am?"

"No, I don't; but I think you are the most lovely lady I have seen."

And the "lovely lady," it is said, blushed deep crimson. . . .

Shy? Yes; and as sensitive to a crude provocation. She can be angry, ragingly angry, and potent in its expression; as is well known to the lady who appeared at Court in a skirt slashed up almost to her knee.

Queen Mary is all things to all women; which is not so much an acquirement as an expression of the full, personal life she has lived—as wife, as mother, as queen. She is not out of her depths, whether the talk is of motherhood or Molière; to hear her in consultation on the subject of trouser patches, how they should be cut, how placed (Miss Bondfield has eloquently borne witness to this) is only just less exhilarating than to hear her drawn out on the subject of Florentine art. She is abreast of modern literature, fiction, memoirs; and by no means unacquainted with the minutes of Trades Union meetings.

She is often said to be "unexpected" in conversation; which means usually that when people meet her for the first time, as for the second or third, she talks about matters that an acutely intelligent person would be expected to talk about. Of course conversation, on the whole, turns on subjects most important to the other person.

At a Labour meeting in Putney, not long ago, a woman associated with the Labour Party was publicly chided for her constant appearances at Court. The last sally came:

"You don't talk politics *there!*"

And, as the lady truthfully as well as indignantly shouted back: "I don't seem to talk anything else!"

"Really," she afterwards explained, "now I come seriously to think of it, I don't think the Queen ever talked to me about anything else outside of Bolshevism —Communism—Socialism—Trades Unionism!"

Precisely!

To-day—to-morrow, she will adventure in some new realm of thought, learning, discovery, in the mood of glow and thrill with which she set out, in the days of long ago at Richmond, on the newest of Ruskin's disquisitions on social reform. And, what is perhaps even more important: "I think I can honestly say," she said only the other day, "that I have never been bored in my life!"

•   •   •   •   •   •   •

More mellowed, more beautiful she grows every day. (Who should have known this better than the late Mlle. Tatry, whose verdict it is? Mlle. Tatry was a just critic rather than an indulgent one, and, having the honour of having "dressed" Princess May in the days of White Lodge, felt strongly that her qualifications as a judge were not to be questioned.) More soft are the blue eyes; and the fair hair of the English Princess is now a coronal of grey which, with that infinite stateliness of all her movements, makes her presence majestic—a Queen every inch of her, a daughter of England.

" 'O Iole, how did you know that Hercules was a god?'

" 'Because,' answered Iole, 'I was content the moment my eyes fell on him!' "

To some women it is given to be loved extravagantly; of few could it be said that the eyes of an Empire have rested on them, and been content.